Looking Past Suffering

STEVEN KIELLEY

I would like to dedicate this book to my wonderful wife and friend, Lisa, who has been my support and traveling partner for these last 42 years.

I have gone through many tough things in my life but the one thing outside of the love and grace of God that has gotten me through was the encouragement and help of my wife.

CONTENTS

FORWARD

The written word comes to life as Author, Pastor, and Chaplain Steven P. Kielley engages us through his gift of descriptive narration. These stories, which are actual events and testimonies, will provide every reader with hope and a glimpse of how, even in our frail humanity, we can discover "wholeness in our brokenness"! By giving the readers a vivid picture of his own life experiences, Steve affirms that as one goes through pain, limitation, suffering and fear, it is a viable and positive discovery to one day say, "Now I See"!

I have personally known Chaplain Steve Kielley for 14 years as ministry colleagues and as Supervisor of Chaplaincy Ministries in our Health Care organization. I, too, can personally attest to his diligence in ministry reflected in his heartfelt and God-given empathy and compassion for others in diverse situations! I have been approached by many families, patients and clients giving accolades to the effect his time and passion has had on them and their loved ones!

I am honored to have been asked to write this Forward and I pray you, too, will feel Steve's true burden to relay the light that will overshadow any difficulties you may be facing!

Rev. Dan M. Geeding, D. Min. BCC

ACKNOWLEDGEMENTS

I would first like to honor the Lord Jesus for His love and faithfulness and His extreme amount of patience as He led me through the many valleys and struggles in my life to the mountain tops of renewal.

Words cannot express nearly enough my gratitude for those special people who have helped me put together this book:

Thanks to Mary Unz and Karen Kassens who have spent many hours going over the editing portion of this manuscript.

To my loving and faithful wife, Lisa, who encouraged me not only as a wife but as a friend to face and walk through the many experiences I share in this book.

I would especially like to thank my brother and best friend, Richard Kielley, who shared some of the challenges he faced in his own walk toward the high calling of Christ.

Also, I'd like to express my gratitude to Tina Leet who showed me how to smile when the storms of life were strong and constant. Tina has also shared a small portion of her own struggles in this book.

I would also like to thank my very close friend and confidant, Dieter Skowron, for not only being the friend he has been through all these years but also for the contribution he has made to this book by sharing his overcoming experience with cancer.

I appreciate and thank my dear friend, Rev. Dan Geeding, who encouraged me in my work as a hospice chaplain, not only as my supervisor, but as a mentor.

PREFACE

As little children, it seems one of the very first words we learned was "Why?"; it came right after the word "No". As we grow older it seems that we become instinctively more curious as to how things exist or even how they originate. This goes beyond the realm of the physical elements of life and into circumstantial things as well. Why did I get sick, why did my dog die, how come no one likes me? The list is virtually as long as time itself.

Some questions have easier answers than others. For instance, as a child I asked, "Where does rain come from?" There was an answer for this question as well as questions such as "Where do babies come from?" Most people would prefer to handle the prior question rather than the latter. However, the answers to questions such as to why people suffer or questions dealing with death are much more difficult to understand.

As Christians we often ask questions in a religious arena. Why does God allow evil when He is good? Why do the righteous have to suffer? Looking inside your own mind I am sure that you have your own list of questions yet to be answered. Unfortunately some questions never do receive an answer. Even as children when we asked our parents the question "Why?" often they would say, "Because I said so!" What does that mean? It means that you have to trust my judgment as I compel you to live under my authority. I never really liked that answer but learned to live with it because I realized my parent's scope of understanding and experience far exceeded mine. The scripture boldly states that "the just shall live by faith". Faith, by biblical definition, is "*made of the substance of things not seen and evidenced by things hoped for.*" Faith then is not based solely on sight or substantial evidence. People who say they will not believe anything that they do not see are virtually saying that their life is solely based on image. That's fine if you know the difference between reality and a mirage. Sight is often deceiving. Things can be manipulated; magicians make a living by controlling what people focus on and perceive.

However, for a Christian faith is a necessity for the essence of God is invisible. The Bible says no man has seen God at any time. God is an omnipresent Spirit that fills all space. We got a glimpse of divinity through Christ as God robed Himself in a body and became a man. Remember, however, that God was not only in that body of Christ but God also still fills all space.

I remember my children constantly bombarding me with questions about this and that. The answers, which at that time in their lives, they would not have been able to comprehend. I would sometimes say, "In due time you will understand; just enjoy the experience", or if it was a bad experience, I would remind them that things constantly change, just like snowflakes; no two days are exactly the same.

So continue to learn and to search for meaning but also realize that some things cannot be comprehended at every given moment of your life. Paul said to the Corinthians, " *For now we see through a glass, darkly; but then face to face: now I know in part; but then shall I know even as also I am known.* " (1 Corinthians 13:12, KJV)

As we read God's Word, the Bible, there will be times God will say - just like your own parents - "Son or daughter of mine, just believe Me; you will understand farther down the line as your own scope of life increases." One day all questions will have a definitive answer, but until then just keep following the map that you have and trust that it will get you to where you need to be.

The purpose of this book is to focus on an age-old question, "Why does God allow the righteous to suffer?" This is certainly the proverbial question of the ages.

Maybe the question should really be, "How should the righteous suffer?" Not "Why do the righteous suffer?" The true character of a man is shown in the way he handles adversity and suffering.

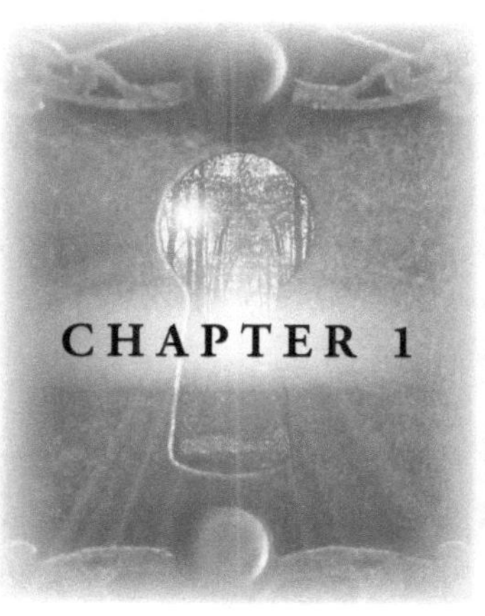

ASKING WHY

Some may say that God does not understand what they are going through. He knows all the answers and sees the end from the beginning. He has never had to ask the question "Why?"- or has He?

We all agree that God was in Christ reconciling the world unto Himself. Most theologians will agree on the point that Jesus Christ was God in the flesh. As God, He was able to walk on water, calm a storm, raise the dead and prophesy of events yet to happen - even His own death. Jesus only lived to 33 years of age. It is believed His stepfather died at an early age and no doubt Jesus, being the eldest son, had to care for His mother, brothers and sisters. Little is known of those early years but you can rest assured that as a young man He faced the same challenges as any other human.

I would like to focus on what happened at the end of His life. We find a badly beaten Christ hanging on a cross; life is slowly ebbing from His body. The pain from the horrendous beating that He had just received accompanied by the horrors and pain He felt as He hung upon the cross was overwhelming. Even as He was dying, Jesus had mercy upon the thief on the cross next to Him and forgave him. Just before He died, the Bible states Jesus cried out with a loud voice and said:

> *"...Eli, Eli, lama sabachthani? that is to say, My God, my God, why hast thou forsaken me?"* (Matthew 27:46, KJV)

I find this very interesting, considering Jesus is both the Son of Man and the Son of God. He dealt with a dual nature. As God, He knew the future and told His disciples of His impending death on the cross. As a man He ate, drank and slept as any other human.

> *"He then began to teach them that the Son of Man must suffer many things and be rejected by the elders, the chief priests and the teachers of the law, and that he must be killed and after three days rise again.* [32] *He spoke plainly about this, and Peter took him aside and began to rebuke him.* [33] *But when Jesus turned and looked at his disciples, he rebuked Peter. "Get behind me, Satan!" he said. "You do not have in mind the concerns of God, but merely human concerns."* [34] *Then he called the crowd to him along with his disciples and said: "Whoever wants to be my disciple must deny themselves and take up their cross and follow me."* (Mark 8:31-34, NIV)

Jesus was familiar with the road to Calvary; it was the reason for the Incarnation. However, knowing something and experiencing it are two different things. Christ asked a question He already had the answer for. Just like we ourselves do when we encounter loss, pain, heartbreak and suffering. Is it wrong to ask the question "Why"? I do not believe it is, however, it is wrong to question the cause for which you are here. I enlisted in the military in 1972. I enlisted in the cause of a nation. The mission was greater than any one man. Some died for the cause of freedom and others lived and countless people have asked the question,

"Why was I spared and others died?" Or "Why was I wounded when others were not?" There was no answer from heaven as Jesus cried out, "*My God, My God, why hast thou forsaken me*?" No angel came down to pull the nails from the cross or heal His many wounds. The sky became like night and the earth shook as the Creator of all things was slain by His own creation. In this book, I want to take you down a path you may have traveled many times, but maybe this time I might be able to show you things around you that you have missed because of your pain and disillusionment with God, with life or with others.

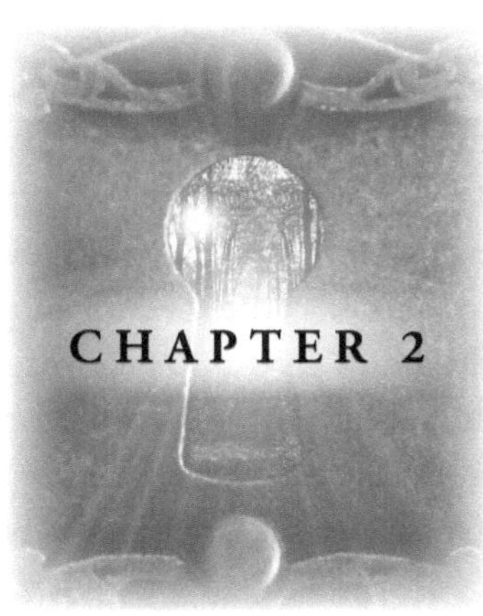

A MAN NAMED GIDEON

Almost 1200 years before the birth of Christ there was a man named Gideon. The man lived at a time when the people of Midian oppressed God's people.

> "*The Israelites did evil in the eyes of the Lord,*
> *and for seven years he gave them into the hands of*
> *the Midianites.* 2 *Because the power of Midian was so*
> *oppressive, the Israelites prepared shelters for themselves*
> *in mountain clefts, caves and strongholds.* 3 *Whenever*
> *the Israelites planted their crops, the Midianites,*
> *Amalekites and other eastern peoples invaded the*
> *country.* 4 *They camped on the land and ruined the*
> *crops all the way to Gaza and did not spare a living*
> *thing for Israel, neither sheep nor cattle nor donkeys.*
> 5 *They came up with their livestock and their tents*
> *like swarms of locusts. It was impossible to count them*
> *or their camels; they invaded the land to ravage it.* 6

Midian so impoverished the Israelites that they cried out to the Lord for help." (Judges 6:1-6, NIV)

Gideon's existence was such that he barely got by and lived literally hand to mouth. It is Gideon that God approached to deliver Israel from the oppression of the Midianites. It is quite interesting how Gideon acted when approached by the God of all the earth and how God addressed Gideon at this first meeting.

> *"The angel of the Lord came and sat down under the oak in Ophrah that belonged to Joash the Abiezrite, where his son Gideon was threshing wheat in a winepress to keep it from the Midianites.* [12] *When the angel of the Lord appeared to Gideon, he said, "The Lord is with you, mighty warrior."*
>
> [13] *"Pardon me, my lord," Gideon replied, "but if the Lord is with us, why has all this happened to us? Where are all his wonders that our ancestors told us about when they said, 'Did not the Lord bring us up out of Egypt?' But now the Lord has abandoned us and given us into the hand of Midian."*
>
> [14] *"The Lord turned to him and said, "Go in the strength you have and save Israel out of Midian's hand. Am I not sending you?"* (Judges 6:11-14, NIV)

At times God views your situation completely differently than you do. Gideon sees himself as a coward hiding as he tries to gain enough sustenance to live from day to day. Notice how God sees him in vs. 12. God sees him as what he can become, not as what he is at the moment. God sees Gideon as a "mighty warrior". Faith changes the lamb into a lion and the meek into a bold aggressor. It's time to change your perception of yourself and see the potential that God has for you if you will walk under the covering of faith.

One of my focuses for writing this book is found in vs. 13. It is the question of the ages, a question we all have asked or will ask at one time or another. "If the Lord is with me, why is all this happening? Why do bad things happen to good people? Why is it that everything seems to be working against me? What have I done to incur the terrible events that are happening in my life or in the lives of those that I love?"

I want to take you on a journey that hopefully will allow you to step outside of your perception of what is going on around you and experience the thrill of what can be if you will live the role that God has called for you to fill. In Gideon's case he can choose to be a warrior or remain a coward. In the story of Gideon we learn that there can be a spiritual metamorphosis that takes place in the midst of struggle. Ask the caterpillar where he changed from a worm to a butterfly and he will tell you it happened in the cocoon of his confinement and physical struggle. New dimensions of life come through the pain of delivery and suffering.

I was born amidst the suffering and pain of my mother's delivery. Your potential for growth is always preceded by struggle and hardship. Of course, we know that Gideon became the warrior he was meant to be and through God's direction and his obedience and bravery he walked through a door that others avoided and delivered Israel from the terrible oppression that they were going through. My goal for you in this journey is for spiritual strength to fill the areas of loss and pain and renew your view of what truly is happening in you and around you. Just as Gideon, you can become a mighty warrior if you will leave your hiding place of hurt and fear.

Remember that God said that David's throne would be an everlasting throne? Revered by the nations and feared by his enemies, David himself wrestled with the question, "WHY?"

> *"How long, LORD? Will you forget me forever? How long will you hide your face from me? [2] How long must I wrestle with my thoughts and day after day have sorrow in my heart? How long will my enemy triumph over me? [3] Look on me and answer, LORD my God. Give light to my eyes, or I will sleep in death, [4] and my enemy will say, "I have overcome him," and*

*my foes will rejoice when I fall. 5 But I trust in your
unfailing love; my heart rejoices in your salvation. 6 I
will sing the LORD's praise, for he has been good to
me." (Psalm 13:1-6, NIV)*

CHAPTER 3

EXPERIENCE IS A GREAT TEACHER

I, at this point, need to give you an idea of my spiritual makeup so as you read these words, you might understand that I am deeply committed to Christ Jesus and truly believe that the Bible is the inspired Word of God.

I graduated from Apostolic Bible College in 1978 and pastored my first church in 1980. I married my wife shortly after I graduated. For the last 42 years, I have pastored churches in a variety of cities. We have seen many people come to Christ under our ministry.

God has been awesome and faithful to us the entire trip. I love the Lord with my whole heart and am aware that He feels the same way about me.

One of our professors in Bible college, Sister Norris, mentioned during one of her lectures, and I quote, "The more I learn about God the more I realize there is so much I don't know." Taking into consideration that she was possibly in her eighties, it caught me off guard.

Just when you feel that you have a handle on this Christian lifestyle, God changes the course of your life. He upsets the apple cart of the familiar and challenges you to know Him in a new dimension. Most people I meet do not like change and are perfectly content to live a normal, uneventful existence.

I have learned that spiritual growth springs up from the soil of struggle. This is easily seen in the early church as it spread across the known world during great persecution and suffering. It seemed that for every Christian killed, 10 more sprang up. The waters of revival only became hot when the fires of persecution, struggle and suffering were turned up. Now I know that we have revivals that pop up amidst us and they burn bright, but in most cases, they settle back down to mediocrity. In this book, I want to focus on the fire and the effects that Christ's life has upon not only our independent lives but on the collective lives of the church body. I do not claim, nor would I, that I am an expert in this field but I do claim to have more association with struggle and pain than what may be considered normal. Possibly, like you, I have lifted up my hands to God asking, "Why God, have all these things come upon me?" My wife and I have on many occasions shed our tears on the cushions of our couch. However, let me state this from the very beginning: every hardship, every struggle, every tear, was worth the growth in our relationship with our Creator. Whether it was a loss of someone we loved, or the betrayal of someone we trusted, or for that matter, the countless struggles with our health. I can honestly say, and my wife would agree, that it brought us to a higher dimension in our relationship with God.

I think that if you were to ask if I had a specialty area in my life, I would quickly answer that it would be with those who are suffering. From early on in my ministry I have worked in hospital chaplaincy. I have, as an employee of a health care system, worked in cancer units, inpatient hospice facilities and home hospice as well. I have been with mothers and dads as they lost their newborn child and in emergency rooms where I stood by parents who held the lifeless bodies of their children. These events have changed me and my heart has more than once been overwhelmed with shared grief. It may have been a spouse who looked with unbelief at their young partner asking the question that has rung through the ages, "Why God?", seeking some reason to justify the loss.

There is another side to this coin that needs to be addressed as well. It is the miraculous side of God. In Mark 16:16 it mentions that "*ye shall pray for the sick and they shall recover.*" Why is it that God heals some and not others? Really, if God is no respecter of persons and He loves everyone alike, why do some receive healing and others, who prayed as hard or harder, continue suffering?

I intend in this book to be very open and transparent. I, like you, have questioned God at the bedside of a family member, pleading with God to touch the diseased body as He has done to countless others and restore to me the one I love.

It was back in 1973 when I became committed to Christ that revival swept through our entire family beginning with my brother and then spreading to me and then my dad and mom. It was a very dramatic change that did not go unnoticed by our relatives or neighbors. We were on fire, so to speak, for God. Up to this time everyone in our family had been relatively healthy. I did lose a younger brother to Sudden Infant Death Syndrome 17 years earlier. But here we were, one big happy bunch, more closely knit together than at any other time in our lives. Then it happened. Dad was diagnosed with lung cancer. Now, I need to let you know something about my dad right from the start. He was my hero, as well as my brother's.

During World War II, he was captured and sent to a German work camp. He was betrayed by one of his own men for stealing flour from a German rail car and then sent to a concentration camp. He was liberated at the end of the war but his body bore the effects of his imprisonment. He was a boxer for the army when he enlisted and was certainly "all man"! Now here he is, laid up in a hospital bed. They have removed one of his lungs and he is not doing very well. Matter of fact, I caught him sharing with my mother what he wanted to happen after his death. Not only did this shatter me and my brother, we were both in our early twenties but it had a direct effect on our newfound faith. I remember asking God, "Why? After all these years of living a sinful and wicked life, why would You take the one that we love right after we have committed our lives to You? Is this our reward for becoming a member of Your family?"

My brother and I were shaken; we knew very little about God or scripture. We had felt God's love but never personally experienced His power. One day as my brother and I were together, we decided to pray for Dad's healing. We saw in the Bible that God often healed and if He did it for one, wouldn't He do it for another? I can remember the day so clearly when my brother and I transformed the family living room into a prayer room. Our prayers that day did not involve folded hands and quiet words. We prayed with all our hearts; the tears flowed as we reached out to our new Friend and Savior, Jesus, asking for His intercession. We did not care about the clock; all that mattered was reaching Jesus and persuading Him to place His healing hand upon our Dad's forehead. Something happened that day. When we left our living room we both felt that God had a plan, that it was going to be alright.

Not only did my dad recover, he was back to driving semi in a short period of time! For the next seven years Dad became a great evangelist to our relatives; he was responsible for helping start a new church in Wisconsin Dells. His testimony was powerful and a good number of our relatives gave their hearts to Jesus. At the end of seven years the cancer was back and this time it would succeed in taking his life.

I need to share one more thing about this. This time as Dad was in the hospital we saw the writing on the wall, so to speak. Dad was calm and ready to go. He gave each of us instructions. Dad was at peace and ready to meet Christ. We each took turns staying with Dad in his room. I remember the night before he died how he seemed to have a turn for the good. He was more awake and alert and seemed to be doing better. We were in Milwaukee at St Luke's Hospital. I decided to run back home to do some work. Little did I know that this would be the day when the Lord would arrive to take him home.

My mother shared this story with us kids. Dad, early in the morning, took a turn for the worse. His breathing changed and his heart raced. As he lay in bed, my mother recounted that he suddenly sat up and looked past her at the wall directly in front of the bed. She mentioned that Dad raised his hands as he reached out and then smiled a great big smile and then passed away. That day my heart broke to think that I would not talk to Dad again in this life. However, my spirit rejoiced in the knowledge that Dad was happy and that he had finished the course on earth that God had assigned to him.

Let me share this thought with you. Back in my early ministry as I worked in the hospital and our missions church, I often asked the question "Why do bad things happen to good people?" I was delighted to find a book that was written with that title and quickly purchased it. Now I will know, I thought, the answer to the age-old question. As I read I became discouraged for it had no answers, only speculations. Many years later as I was reading my Bible I came across this verse that Paul wrote shortly before his death.

> 7 "*I have fought a good fight, I have finished my course, I have kept the faith:* 8 *Henceforth there is laid up for me a crown of righteousness, which the Lord, the righteous judge, shall give me at that day: and not to me only, but unto all them also that love his appearing.*" (2 Timothy 4:7-8, KJV)

The beginning of the verse jumped off the page to me so to speak. Paul knew the end was nearing and like a good dad, he was preparing his son in the Lord for what was about to happen. He says to Timothy, "*I have finished my course.*" I said to God, "Okay, what is it You want me to see?" I looked at the word 'course' and began to let my imagination go. I saw golf courses; I saw mini golf; I saw 9 hole golf courses; I saw 18 hole golf courses. I saw professional courses that were extremely difficult and others that were so very short and simple. It was then that I saw the meaning. Everyone in this life is assigned their own course. Some are short and do not last long; others are not as hard and some are very difficult. The better players always ended up on the harder courses, usually because they became more practiced in the game. They had graduated from one course to another. Your course may be easy or it may be hard. What is important is that you give the game all that you have. When you have completed the last hole, so to speak, the game will be over. No one knows when the last hole is coming up but rest assured, as Paul said, you also will finish your course.

I look at my brother who was born from the same father and mother, yet our lives outside of being the same in Christ are so radically different. I used to say, "God, why must I battle all these diseases? They are like summer storms; one follows the other. Why can't I be like others who seem to have a normal, non-eventful life when it comes to health?" My brother has always been healthy. I used to tease him. Actually, I still tease him and ask him if mom was taking drugs while she was pregnant with me that I ended up with all these health problems. Now I clearly see that God sent me these trials to prepare me for the ministry that He had in store for me. I truly share empathy and compassion with those I minister to because of the struggles I myself have faced.

Remember what Paul said in Romans 8:

> "*And we know that all things work together for good to them that love God, to them who are the called according to His purpose.*" (Romans 8:28, KJV)

I have to point out to you that the word 'purpose' at the end of the verse is preceded by the word 'His' and not the word 'your'! God has a purpose for your life; you were designed to fit into the picture that God is painting. Rest assured, God has a special place for you in His plan; it may not be the one you choose but it will be the best one collectively for His purpose.

> "*Take, my brethren, the prophets, who have spoken in the name of the Lord, for an example of suffering affliction, and of patience.* [11] *Behold, we count them happy which endure. Ye have heard of the patience of Job, and have seen the end of the Lord; that the Lord is very pitiful, and of tender mercy.*" (James 5:10-11, KJV)

CHAPTER 4

THE PATIENCE OF JOB HAS A LIMIT

The wind stirs the trees outside the window. The fragrance of the blossoms that grow in abundance on its branches provide a feast of fragrance to Job as he stirs on this sunny morning. "It is another wonderful time to be alive!", he whispers to no one in particular. He goes about the morning tasks as he prepares to embrace the events of the day. Job's wife smiles to herself as she hears him whistling outside their dwelling. "Job is such an optimist.", she muses to no one in particular, "always grateful for the many blessings that others would not so readily notice." His seven sons and three wonderful daughters are the diamonds of life, each one of them holding a very special place in his heart. He is very well respected in the Land of Uz and many seek his counsel.

Little does Job realize that today would be the day that would change the course of his life. Today he would face the peak of blessing and be cast down to the depths of despair and suffering.

I stand amazed each time I pick up this wonderful book we call the Bible. For each time I thumb through its pages, it reaches out to me and reveals its hidden secrets. The writings of this book make me think and expand my view of this great cosmos that surrounds us. Each book points to the awesomeness of God and His love for humanity. However, there are special times when I read that I find myself standing next to the person on the page. On this particular day, I find myself standing next to a man named Job. He is a greatly respected man when we first meet. He certainly is a scholar, very wise and enlightened to the realm of God's reign. He is very humble and connected to his family. His heart is attached to each of his children and grandchildren. He loves to watch them laugh and grow. Proud papa he is! Of course, like most children, they have their challenges and make at times, questionable, if not really bad decisions. However, Job has patience with each. Every day he surrounds each family member with a wall of prayer, asking God to protect and forgive each of his children for any action they may have taken contrary to the will of God.

In the scope of scripture, Job fits into a divine format of growth; the Book of Job shows us how to suffer, just as the Book of Psalms teaches us how to pray. In like manner the Book of Proverbs tells us how to act and the Book of Ecclesiastes how to enjoy life or rejoice and the Song of Solomon how to love. Each of these aspects strengthens the spiritual character of man.

That is certainly the question Job raises, but it is worthy to note that Job himself never receives a direct answer or even an indirect one for that matter, nor is one given by the author. However, scripture informs of the answer to satan's challenge, "Does Job fear God for nothing?" I repeat the same question for your consideration. Does man fear God for nothing? The scriptures allow us to be privy to the challenge of satan as it is given in heaven. We are also made aware that God allows Job to suffer in answer to that challenge but Job is never told of this. Job's life certainly does not go unnoticed in heaven for Job's integrity and compassion and faithfulness shines like a lighthouse amidst the darkness of man's depravity.

To say that God loved Job would be an understatement. God enjoys each moment that He walks by the side of this earthly human friend named Job. He certainly feels the integrity that follows each decision that he makes. Papas love to brag about their children and in this case, God cannot refrain as He points Job out to a very dubious-looking character called satan.

It seems that heaven is the epicenter of God's existence, the White House of the galaxies, and everything stands under its authority. Satan is the epitome of evil and why God would showcase Job in front of such a character at first is not easily understood. Don't think for a moment that satan has not already been watching Job himself. He hates Job nearly as much as he hates God. He taunts him every chance he gets, but satan points out to God at their interview in heaven that God withholds him from touching Job or causing him any harm. How frustrating and aggravating it is, he explains; it's like putting a muzzle on a fox and letting him into the hen house. God smiles at satan for he certainly must enjoy his frustration, for he at one time had shared God's attention and honor. He could not hold onto humility and was swept into the current of self-glorification with a lot of different ripples of pride. That pride was now bubbling inside as he watched Job's Creator boast about this one who walked with God with a humble spirit and a love for his Creator as satan himself had once done. Look at the scripture where God speaks to satan about Job:

> *"Then the Lord said to Satan, "Have you considered My servant Job, that there is none like him on the earth, a blameless and upright man, one who fears God and shuns evil?"* (Job 2:3, NKJV)

God asked a question that He knew the answer to. Job was a thorn in satan's side; Job was a beacon of light that revealed his own failures. However, I ask the question, "Why does it seem as if God is firing up satan?" It was like jabbing a sleeping bear or stepping on the tail of a cat. Why is God focusing satan on Job? Satan is telling God that Job is only a faithful servant because of the blessings and protection that He supplies. It's then that God does something so profound and outside the walls of man's spiritual reasonings; He begins to tear down the hedge that has protected Job. God is allowing evil to not only linger outside the perimeter of Job's life but to touch it.

> *"There was a man in the land of Uz, whose name was Job; and that man was blameless and upright, and one who feared God and shunned evil. 2 And seven sons and three daughters were born to him. 3 Also, his possessions were seven thousand sheep, three thousand camels, five hundred yoke of oxen, five hundred female donkeys, and a very large household, so that this man was the greatest of all the people of the East."*
>
> *4 "And his sons would go and feast in their houses, each on his appointed day, and would send and invite their three sisters to eat and drink with them. 5 So it was, when the days of feasting had run their course, that Job would send and sanctify them, and he would rise early in the morning and offer burnt offerings according to the number of them all. For Job said, "It may be that my sons have sinned and cursed God in their hearts." Thus Job did regularly.*
>
> *6 Now there was a day when the sons of God came to present themselves before the LORD, and Satan also came among them. 7 And the LORD said to Satan, "From where do you come? So Satan answered the LORD and said, "From going to and fro on the earth, and from walking back and forth on it." 8 Then the LORD said to Satan, "Have you considered My servant Job, that there is none like him on the earth, a blameless and upright man, one who fears God and shuns evil?"*
>
> *9 So Satan answered the LORD and said, "Does Job fear God for nothing? 10 Have You not made a hedge around him, around his household, and around all that he has on every side? You have blessed the work*

> *of his hands, and his possessions have increased in the land. [11] But now, stretch out Your hand and touch all that he has, and he will surely curse You to Your face!"* (Job 1:1-11, NKJV)

Over time not only have I experienced the distinct feeling that if I pray and am not healed instantly that my faith is lacking or I have some spiritual defect that is holding God back from doing what I have so desperately asked Him to do. This thought has been bred into many through several scriptures that denote that Jesus healed all the sick that came to Him. That the scriptures imply healing is according to a person's faith and that it is God's will for none to suffer or to be sick or have pain. It is also many times implied that disease and illness is brought about by a person's lack of righteousness. As in the case of Job and his friends accusations against his integrity which they implied brought about his physical suffering. This seems to be contrary to scriptures and instances where God allowed adversity and pain for spiritual benefit. As was in the case of Paul asking for God's healing and God denying his request. God encouraged Paul that through his suffering that God's strength could be made perfect in his life. Paul shares therefore that he will glory in his infirmities for when he is weak yet he is strong.

As we continue, we will find Job's friends confronting Job and using these principles of prosperity and protection through one's actions to justify a life without hardship and continual blessing. "It is your fault Job; you are suffering because of what you have secretly done that has offended God." Is it possible that Job is a type of the Church, and that God points the body of believers out to satan, and satan in the same sense, accuses God that His Church only serves Him for the benefits and protection He supplies?

As we explore the Book of Job, put yourself in Job's place. Feel the initial surprise as he loses the security of his wealth and then the children he so dearly loves. The question we may ask is, "If God is a loving God and has the power to protect and provide and prosper those He loves and He does not do it, could it be a reflection of some defect in His character that denotes a lesser love than we had believed?" Man is very good at making God into his own image. However, you cannot put God into a mold and reshape Him. For what mold could contain Him, what knowledge that we possess is able to discern the depths of His character and understanding?

The story of Job is one of the oldest writings in scripture. I believe God from the very beginning wanted those who walked with Him to not solely put their trust in life's circumstances, for the situations of life change from moment to moment. God is reaching out to you and me, wanting each of us to see the greater picture. The Book of Job is like watching a train run off the tracks, each car tumbling down the embankment, one after the other. With no way to stop it, you become as a spectator helplessly watching the calamity as it continues until the last car joins the carnage. I feel that atheists use this example the most in theorizing the nonexistence of God. If God was good, why would He allow evil to continue? I believe the answer lies in the Book of Job.

Now I consider myself a somewhat loving father; I would do anything to help my kids if they were suffering. If they were in pain I would do everything within my power to help the pain go away. Am I a better father than my heavenly Father?

Dad was always watching out for me, whether it be a physical illness or emotional struggle, he was always there to support me. Oftentimes he could not take away the pain or heal the hurt but his presence provided the support for me to face the challenge. Some time ago I requested my military records. I remember opening up the manilla envelope and looking at the information that was sent. It was then I found a letter that was enclosed in these records which were sent back to me addressed to my commanding officer. It read, to be brief, "Please watch over my son." I look back now and realize that there were probably many times Dad had gone behind the scenes to look out for me. I remember how I would get upset with him when I needed financial help and even though he could have relieved my burden, he withheld the help. I look back all these years and thank him for refraining from many of my petitions. The greatest gift that he ever gave me was the gift of confidence and endurance. He provided within me a work ethic that has allowed me to go on when everything around me was trying to persuade me to quit.

Job never hears the discussion going on in heaven. To Job, it's another day not unlike many others. Hell's doors are about to open and an army of demons are going to swarm around this placid picture.

Can you see Job as the first servant shares his news?

> "*and a messenger came to Job and said, "The oxen were plowing and the donkeys feeding beside them, [15] when the Sabeans raided them and took them away—indeed they have killed the servants with the edge of the sword; and I alone have escaped to tell you*!" (Job 1:14-15, NKJV)

"Master it was a day like any other, the fields were being worked and all was peaceful when the enemy came. They're all gone; it's lost!" The unexpectedness of tragedy or loss is the most difficult loss.

We often do not get to choose the time of our testing. The torrents of pain and struggle fall upon us without mercy as we fall to our knees and look to heaven for answers and hope. Satan always will allow at least one to survive to bring the news of devastation, like striking concrete blow after blow waiting for it to break apart from the inside out.

Satan's assault on Job was precisely planned to not allow him to regenerate or recover from the previous assault. "*While he was still speaking, another also came and said, "The Chaldeans formed three bands, raided the camels and took them away, yes, and killed the servants with the edge of the sword; and I alone have escaped to tell you!" [18] While he was still speaking, another also came and said, "Your sons and daughters were eating and drinking wine in their oldest brother's house, [19] and suddenly a great wind came from across the wilderness and struck the four corners of the house, and it fell on the young people, and they are dead; and I alone have escaped to tell you*!" (Job 1:17-19, NKJV)

Scripture mentions that all these attacks by satan came at the same time in a well-planned manner. Even nature attacked the hopes and dreams of Job's blessings.

As I stated earlier for many years I have worked in the healthcare field. My first position was as a Hospital Chaplain. I watched the raw and overwhelming grief of moms and dads as they held the bodies of their lifeless children. In some cases, it was a day like any other day and they died suddenly and unexpectedly. There was no preparation for loss or grief; it came in like a tsunami, ripping away joy and leaving devastation and feelings of raw and uncontrolled grief in its wake.

This cannot be a coincidence, Job thought to himself. Like all of us, Job went to the source of his meaning, to the core of his existence for reasoning. God must be doing this to me. Satan wanted Job to think this way, for if he can destroy Job's view of God's compassion and love, he can break him away from his loyalty and faithfulness. He feels he can actually take away his reason for existence and his will to continue to live. Remember, all these things happened in a very short period of time.

I now see a broken man shattered by the torrents of devastation and loss. He can get over the loss of oxen and camels, he can get over the loss of structures and achievements, but he is struggling with the loss of those he loves and those he felt responsible for; his children and his servants were under his care. Satan learns, however, that even though he has struck a crippling blow he has not snuffed out the candle of Job's trust. The flames flick back and forth but it still remains bright.

> "*Then Job arose, tore his robe, and shaved his head; and he fell to the ground and worshiped.* [21] *And he said: "Naked I came from my mother's womb, And naked shall I return there. The LORD gave, and the LORD has taken away; Blessed be the name of the LORD."*
>
> [22] *In all this Job did not sin nor charge God with wrong.*" (Job 1:20-22, NKJV)

TINA'S STORY

A number of years ago I had the distinct pleasure of getting to know Tina, a young lady in our church, and her mother Carol. Carol had already lost her husband and of course, Tina had lost her dad. Death in any circumstance is very difficult to deal with but both Tina and Carol had found strength and faith to face this challenge in their lives through their relationship with God. From the very beginning I need to tell you that these two are inseparable, not only in their relationship as mother and daughter but also as best friends. Tina's loss of her dad had a profound impact on her as she grew into adulthood.

She was 18 years old, young, vibrant and ready to face not only the challenges of life but she also wanted to grow in independence. In 2005 she enlisted in the Navy. While in the Navy she worked on the maintenance of helicopters.

Tina's athletic ability allowed her to enjoy many different activities - snowboarding was one of them. In 2008 while on leave, during one of her snowboarding adventures, she had taken a spill and injured her right knee, but she recovered from it. Thus, she was able to continue on with activities until another accident took place.

While performing maintenance on a helicopter, she fell from the helicopter sustaining serious injuries to the same knee. This injury along with the previous snowboarding knee injury would come into play and change her life.

Not only had she torn her sciatic nerve in half, but she was now diagnosed with a condition called CRPS (Complex Regional Pain Syndrome). In April 2009, she was airlifted to Balboa Hospital in San Diego, California. Not only was her body racked with pain but now she began having seizures. After about a year and a half Tina found herself totally disabled and confined to a wheelchair. This attractive young woman's life had been totally transformed; she had lost the use of one of her legs. The nerve disorder was so serious that if the leg was even touched she would immediately go into a seizure. To wash and clean her leg she would have to be put under general anesthetic. I have asked her to share part of her journey with you so what you are about to read next are her words. I must point out that I do not know a more inspiring and loving person than Tina. Of course, I cannot begin to share the multitude of complications that she deals with daily but I can share with you that she is the most optimistic person I have ever met! Yes, she does have her dark days, but her resiliency to bounce back can only come through the things she has learned on her own journey through the valley of suffering and her faith in Jesus Christ.

Tina's Story: *Have you ever felt totally alone? Like no one could ever understand? You are left in a world of pain to suffer all alone with no one to share and support your feelings; they can't help you though because they don't understand. It is so very hard to find people with true empathy and understanding to relate to what you are going through.*

See, these were my feelings; I was left all alone to just suffer and die with my own pain and diagnoses. I was just suffering silently underneath a shell that I put up around me, faking that everything was fine every time

I had to go out in public or even to the doctor. I now look back and I am dumbfounded that I did this and that I thought my life was over.

See, the thing that you don't realize at the time is that God puts someone in your path every now and again who reaches out to help lift you up from your despair. If you aren't careful to realize it, the comfort and encouragement that someone can share with you can quickly just pass you by. While at the Naval Hospital it always seemed like after my most painful doctor appointments, while I was heading back to my room, God would always put someone in my path to lift me up and encourage me. A couple of times it was an invite to lunch and other times it was a hug and a word of encouragement. Those words of encouragement seemed like they were always sincere but I was never told that everything would be ok. The words that were most often spoken were, "You can get through this day!" or "Remember, you are not forgotten!" Those words meant so much and I connected to them with a hug. It would put a smile back on my face, which in turn, lifted my spirits. I would tell myself, "Don't give up, keep fighting, you are well-loved!" Then I would go back to my room and read the Book of Job.

That has become one of my favorite books in the Bible because I feel Job's pain and suffering. I feel like I don't just relate to Job but that God has Job relate to me and my pain and suffering. In a way, it is like God has empathy and shows His empathy to me through the suffering that Job had gone through. For instance, like Job, his friends were no help at all and most likely made Job feel even more alone with his pain and suffering. I have even had those who I thought were my closest friends, the ones that were there for me when I lost my dad at 15 years old, leave me and not talk to me anymore because I am in a wheelchair, have lots of pain and have seizures every now and again when the pain gets too much for my body to handle. It still baffles me to this day on how my closest friends could be there for me when my dad died but now since I am injured, they do not want anything to do with me.

Again, that is where I have found God's light and goodness come in and take over with His love and comfort! God put new friends in my path who needed to be loved and encouraged as well! This never would have happened if I hadn't gotten injured and had not gone through this pain and suffering! See, you can look at your pain and suffering, I feel, in two different ways. The first way is to be like Job's wife, refuse God, stay in your pit and suffer all alone and die that way, which I think, no one wants or would want. The second way is to say, "Ok God, please change my attitude and perspective and let me see with Your eyes the people that I can reach out to and touch, whether it be with just a smile or a simple word of encouragement." Your pain may not lessen but you do begin to realize you are not alone and also end up being comforted, having a better attitude and outlook on life. Before you know it you are living what you can feel is a full life. It is so rewarding and encouraging to be able to share your pain and suffering as I have and I hope you will too!!!

May God Bless You! Tina

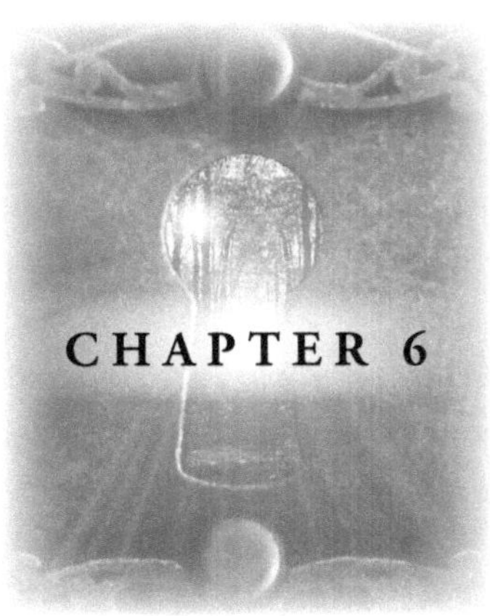

CHAPTER 6

DOES HEAVEN'S RESTRAINT WORK FOR OUR GREATER GOOD?

Have you ever been there, feeling the claws of uncertainty digging into your heart? Have you ever felt the curtain close on hope and feel the desperation of calamity after calamity? It seems that your mind and heart cannot process the grief and you find yourself overwhelmed. I remember some years ago, Lisa and I were living in a little town called Temperanceville, located in Virginia. It was my first church; it was a lovely church with lovely people and a thriving school. Our road to this endeavor started in Salt Lake City at a conference. We had met another minister from Delaware who was overseeing several churches that were seeking pastors. He invited me to fly out and visit each to see if I might be interested in ministering in one of them. This I did, and to make a long story short, I decided on a church in Hallwood, VA which is on the Eastern Shore of Chesapeake Bay. We loaded up the truck, quit our jobs in Milwaukee and headed for the Eastern Shore. That was the beginning of calamity. From the beginning everything started to go wrong. Even on the drive there I suffered from food poisoning. When we finally arrived, our accommodations turned out to be a mobile home miles from the church. We used to shiver as we watched the wind blow our curtains on cold nights; that was with the windows closed!

The church did very well but we found out afterward that there was to be no compensation for our efforts. Yes, we had been misled. The church was more than able to cover our expenses and salaries but all monies were funneled into the host's church. We gradually spent all of our savings. My wife was able to find a part-time job a number of miles away but we could not survive and headed toward complete poverty. I searched for extra work everywhere but it seemed in this area jobs were scarce. I even tried to get a job at Purdue working in chicken processing and was told I was overqualified.

We were desperate; the church people were nice and helped as they were able. I cried out to God, "Lord don't You see me down here, don't You care? I have come to do Your work and I feel like I have been disowned."

Then it happened early one morning. I was to meet with the parents of a child wanting to enroll in our school and I was running late. I jumped in our junker and as I was hurriedly backing down the driveway it happened. I learned by accident that there was a leech bed right next to the driveway. A leach bed is connected to the sewer system and used for drainage. When I drove off the driveway the rear tire went into the leach bed and sunk down to the axle. Here I was in my one nice suit, late for my appointment, stuck in a lake of sewage. It was more than I could take; everywhere I turned everything was against me or so it seemed. I was mad; I was disappointed with God. I then did a very foolish thing. I opened the door and leaned out looking at the rear tire. I put the transmission in reverse and put the gas pedal to the floor. I do not know what I expected to happen but I can tell you what did! The tire sprayed sewage all over my exposed body, from the top of my head to my waist!

Now I have shared this story because at this point something inside of me broke. I looked at my hands, my clothes, the inside of my car, and it was like I was drained of all emotion. I was numb. I got out of the car, walked into the trailer and sat on the couch. I mouthed the words, "Lord I give up! Tell me what it is that You want me to do?" It was then that the Lord spoke to me and told me to go back home. I had never really included Him in my plans of coming to this city. Oh sure, I told Him how good of a situation I thought it would be and how great a pastor I could be, but He had not sent me. It had been my wife's and my decision. We learned an important lesson, that there is a difference between a need and a call. Of course, we hardly had any money to buy gas, much less rent a truck and bring our meager belongings back to her parent's home where we would start all over again. Oh, by the way, guess who we found out was now pregnant? Hint, it wasn't me!

I know this in no way compares to what Job went through but he no doubt was wondering just as I, why everything was falling apart. Where is God in my suffering? Where is God in my pain? We all ask these questions at one time or another. God sees every tear, He catches each one in His hand.

> "*You have seen me tossing and turning through the night. You have collected all my tears and preserved them in your bottle! You have recorded every one in your book.*" (Psalm 56:8, TLB)

I see Job with his hands reached up to heaven; I hear the mournful cry and as it escapes his lips, it comes from the deepest part of his being. However, he retains his integrity and does not blame God falsely at this time.

Satan, however, will not stop here. He never stops until he gets what he wants. He will keep coming back looking for every opportunity. However, satan has a chain that only allows him to go so far.

Most people never stop to think of what God was experiencing as these events unfolded. Do you think He watched impassively while Job faced wave after wave of testing? Do you think that He was oblivious to his grief and watched idly as the one He loved faced all these losses? Do you think that you are a better father than He is? I remember learning a lesson some time back. My daughter was finishing her last year of college at the UW of Whitewater. The college was close enough so that she could live at home and commute each day. However, it was late one Friday night and as I laid in bed waiting for the downstairs door to open, I realized it was nearly one o'clock in the morning. She never got home this late without letting me know where she was. In my mind I saw every possible calamity parade before my eyes. Abductions, auto accidents and the list went on. I prayed in my concern, "God please take care of my daughter wherever she is." It was then I heard God speak very clearly to me. He said "She was my daughter before she was yours. Do you think for one moment that you are a better father than me?"

I felt foolish to think that I had to plead with God to take care of one of His own children, whom He adores, the ones He loves. How would I feel if someone asked me to watch over and take care of my daughter? I would say much the same thing and more than likely you would too. God watched these events and no doubt, had to restrain Himself from interfering with what was taking place.

God watched Christ as He suffered on the cross. Not only God, but all heaven's forces had to refrain themselves from interfering with this divine act of love and compassion. Where would the world be today without the blood atoning sacrifice of the cross? Don't think for a moment that God is complacent when it comes to you either. Don't think for one moment that He does not feel your infirmities or sense your pain and struggle with a heart bigger than time and space.

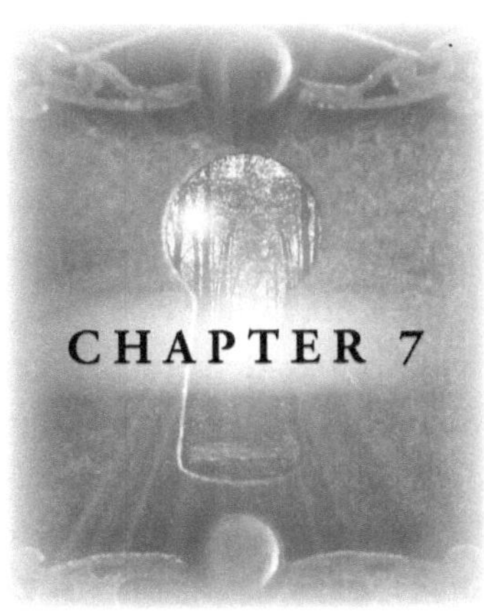

THE BLESSING OF PAIN

Have you ever wondered why God created pain? With all the amazing feelings that our five senses can process, why must there be pain? I remember reading a story sometime ago of a request a mother made for her daughter. The mother was being interviewed and the last statement she made in the interview is this: "My prayer for my daughter every night is, 'Dear God, please let my daughter feel pain.'" This, without knowing the history of the situation, would be a very strange prayer request indeed. Who would ever want someone they loved, especially a child, to experience pain and actually pray for it to happen? You will understand when I tell you the rest of the story. This woman's daughter has a rare disease that does not allow her to feel physical pain. This is a rare disease called CIPA (congenital insensitivity to pain with anhidrosis). Very few people have ever contracted this disease in all of human history.

A life without pain at first would seem quite appealing to us, that is until we realize that pain serves a major purpose in our existence. How would you know if you stepped on a nail or if a pan was hot if you could not feel the pain? How would you have a preemptive warning of something that was wrong in your body if there were no pain or discomfort? I am one of those unfortunate guys who has developed a long-lasting relationship with his dentist. I usually have a warning of tooth decay evidenced by a toothache. If the pain gives me an early warning sign, there is a good chance that the dentist will be able to destroy the decay and save the tooth.

Pain is not pleasant and uncontrolled pain can be overwhelming. However, a life without it would be dangerous. In a moral sense, pain is like our conscience. If we violate a spiritual principle our conscience, if it is working, will produce an unpleasant feeling called guilt, which will cause the side effects of restlessness and sorrow.

It is hard for us to comprehend, in the case of Job, not only the emotional aspect of his suffering but also the physical part of his suffering. Satan was given permission to take Job to the edge of death but could not take his life. Job described his appearance and the physical struggle of his pain and torment. Let's look at Job 2 and see a snapshot of this next challenge:

> *"Then the LORD said to Satan, "Have you considered My servant Job? For there is no one on earth like him—blameless and upright, fearing God and shunning evil. He still retains his integrity, even though you incited Me against him to ruin him without cause."*
>
> *4 "Skin for skin!" Satan replied. "A man will give up all he owns in exchange for his life. 5 But stretch out Your hand and strike his flesh and bones, and he will surely curse You to Your face." 6 "Very well," said the LORD to Satan. "He is in your hands, but you must spare his life."*
>
> *7 "So Satan went out from the presence of the LORD and infected Job with terrible boils from the soles of his feet to the crown of his head. 8 And Job took a piece of broken pottery to scrape himself as he sat among the ashes."* (Job 2:3-8, NIV)

Let me prefix my next remarks by making this statement: there are a good many people that can stand considerable challenges, but very few who can achieve when physical health and enormous pain are heaped on top of many already heavy burdens. Satan had a plan and it would have succeeded, no doubt, on a good many people but the fabric of Job's existence was not solely intertwined with the fluctuating circumstances of human life. Job's life was intertwined with that of God. Satan had another card to play in his hand; he no doubt thought that this card would be the trump card which would cause Job to throw up his hands and curse God. It was the one thing that is closest to the heart of man more than anything else and that is his wife, his helpmate, his soulmate and confidant. I have gone through many tough things in my life but the one thing outside of the love and grace of God that has gotten me through was the encouragement and help of my wife. This, however, was going to be taken from Job just as everything else of value in this situation.

> Please note this verse: "*His wife said to him, "Are you still maintaining your integrity? Curse God and die*!" (Job 2:9, NIV)

Satan clasped his hands together and a sneer came over his dark and evil face, but to his surprise Job stood tall, facing this attack on his integrity and the pain of betrayal from the wife he loved so dearly.

> "*He replied, You are talking like a foolish woman. Shall we accept good from God, and not trouble?" In all this, Job did not sin in what he said*." (Job 2:10, NIV)

It was at this point Job began to feel alone; amidst a world full of people he felt as though he was an island lost in a turbulent sea with no sense of direction or hope of deliverance.

There was no shoulder for him to cry on, no one to speak faith and hope. Job's only hope was in God and at present, even though he had stood firm to this point, he could feel the foundation shaking under his feet, for this pain, this loss, these insurmountable events made no sense. Oh, if only Job's eyes could have seen and his ears could have heard the events that were taking place in heaven! How he would have gathered his strength and resolve and would not have wavered.

Job looked at his boil-covered body and the weeping of his wounds and the itching and painful discomfort that cried out for attention from every part of his body. He smelled the stench, he saw the swelling and oozing of each boil. The flies buzzed around his body as they would a corpse lying on the ground. There was no break from his torment, no moment of peace, sleep was impossible and his strength was ebbing away due to the fever he bore. His wife had departed from him and left him to his suffering. How could the beauty of the day so drastically have changed in such a short time? How truly fickle life had been, like a deceitful lover, he now was left alone.

Oh that God would come to him and share the reason for his torment, to bring some sense to suffering. His mouth and mind were filled with questions, each demanding their own answer, yet the world around him was silently taunting his condition.

Some questions one might ask are: What benefit does a person get from suffering? What gain can there be from loss? How can a person prosper when they lose their health, their perspective and purpose? How can a bird sing when it cannot fly, or bees produce honey without the beauty of the blossoms? What good thing can come forth from Job's misery? Why would God allow one He loves so much to descend into the pit of despair and hopelessness? Is it that God takes joy in our suffering; would not that make Him somewhat sadistic? Is it that God does not care? After all, what does man have to offer that God does not already possess? These trials of life, however, seem to come like the storms of summer, blasting in with all their fury and veracity. I do not think any of those things which I have spoken are true, quite to the contrary. I believe God feels every part of our desperation and pain and it is in these times He shows His wisdom and strength as He lifts us above the pit of despondency.

There once was a man named Paul; you may have met him when he was named Saul. He was a man of Tarsus, a prominent Roman theologian, very highly educated and learned in Jewish law. He was passionate and zealous when it came to God and His ways. We could actually say that he was very religious. He had a bull dog's tenacity and the porcupine's prickability. Paul was too close to himself to see his true condition and relationship to God. Even though Saul felt he was a great Patriarch of the law, little did he know that he was fighting the very cause that he claimed to be helping. The whole message of the law pointed to the Christ who would break down the doors of death and hell and free man from the shackles of death. However, before his eyes could ever see, they must first be blinded. Let's look more closely at Paul's story in scripture.

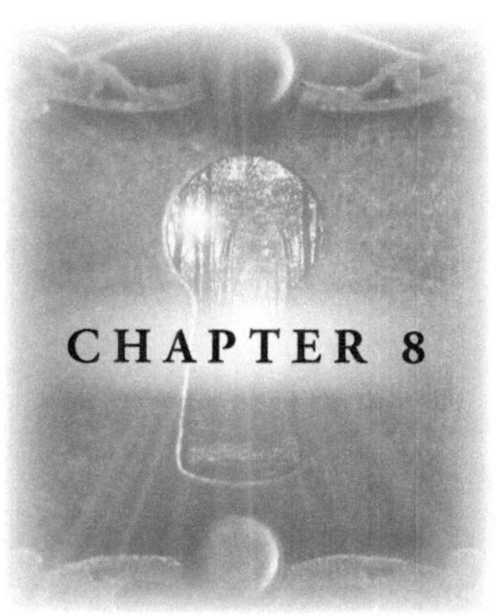

CHAPTER 8

FROM SAUL TO PAUL ... A CHANGE OF HEART AND NAME

*"Meanwhile, Saul was still breathing out mur-
derous threats against the Lord's disciples. He went to
the high priest* 2 *and asked him for letters to the syn-
agogues in Damascus, so that if he found any there
who belonged to the Way, whether men or women,
he might take them as prisoners to Jerusalem.* 3 *As he
neared Damascus on his journey, suddenly a light from
heaven flashed around him.* 4 *He fell to the ground
and heard a voice say to him, "Saul, Saul, why do you
persecute me?"*

5 *"Who are you, Lord?" Saul asked. "I am Jesus,
whom you are persecuting," he replied.* 6 *"Now get up
and go into the city, and you will be told what you
must do."*

7 *"The men traveling with Saul stood there
speechless; they heard the sound but did not see anyone.*

> [8] *Saul got up from the ground, but when he opened his eyes he could see nothing. So they led him by the hand into Damascus.* [9] *For three days he was blind, and did not eat or drink anything.*" (Acts 9:1-9, NIV)

If Saul was ever to be the man that God was calling him to be, there had to be a confrontation. He fell to the earth and covered his face to hide from this One who spoke from heaven. The question that is asked by Saul is very interesting and very revealing. He asks, "Who are you Adonai?" This is a name for God. Saul, are you not a learned theologian? Have you not been schooled in the scriptures from your youth? Certainly you have shared your knowledge with others as to who and what God is.

As he lay on the ground humbled before his peers, a door opens into his mind and his heart and the light of conviction reveals his lack of knowledge and experience. The One whom he was fighting against was the very One to whom he claimed allegiance. A man who thought he had sight now is blind and his blindness will take him to a place of revelation and change.

So powerful was this visitation and confrontation that Saul neither ate nor drank for three days and his sight did not return until Christ came to him again. How he must have felt, all his dreams and aspirations lay in the dust on the road to Damascus. He realized he did not know God even in a minute way. However, Saul was going to rise from the dust of confusion and when he does he will be a completely changed person with a vision of God others might not ever experience. A complete transformation was taking place in this darkened room on a street called Straight.

Sometimes we have to be brought down to make us look upward. There are fruits that grow on the tree of suffering that you can find nowhere else. They provide enlightenment, endurance and maturity. These attributes are not found in books and can only be achieved through renewed faith and godly trust.

CHAPTER 9

MY WHOLE LIFE IS A CONTROLLED BURN

I am fortunate to live near some very lovely state forests. It seems every spring as I wind down Highway 67, I will come across signs which make this statement: "You are entering into an area of a controlled burn. Please do not call 911." I thought the State Parks Commission was established to protect our forests. Why in the world would you start a fire in a forest that you were sent to protect? It seems that over time, so I'm told, if vegetation is not thinned out, there will be no new growth. The old must yield to the flames so that new growth can continue.

As I thought on this topic, I began to realize that in my life God has controlled burns quite regularly. I see things that I once cherished go up in flames and I see the smoke of their passing. I have learned after these times to look for the new life that will replace what is gone. Gone are my parents, many of my aunts, uncles and a brother and a sister, yet around me I see the new faces of my children and grandchildren. Yes, the pain of their passing lingers on. A question I have often been asked by my patients is, "How long will I feel the pain of grief?" I sincerely answer, "As long as love exists in a person's heart, the grief of loss will linger."

My dad's passing happened nearly thirty years ago and honestly, there is not a day that I do not bring back and hold the memories of his being present with me. Each memory is like a precious diamond, each with its own shape and clarity. Sometimes they make me laugh and at other times they bring tears of longing. However, I would not exchange these little diamonds for anything because not only do they draw my thoughts back to what has been but they also refocus my thoughts to what is coming. How marvelous a gift God has given each of us to hold onto in the midst of loss and uncertainty.

CHAPTER 10

FROM DECEIVER TO CONTENDER ... THE STORY OF CHANGE

I remember a man named Jacob, a man of somewhat good intentions when I first met him in the Book of Genesis, but yet he was a man of a somewhat dubious character. He was a man that would stop at nothing to get what he wanted and would use lies and deceit to achieve his purpose. Even though his intentions were good, his methods were certainly not above reproach. His actions resulted in him fleeing from his home and family and residing with relatives in a place called Haran. It was there he began to grow spiritually and develop a life that was disciplined and reputable. God had given him visions and promises during his expulsion and like Job, he became extremely wealthy not only in flocks and herds but also with family.

One day in a dream God directed Jacob to return home and under God's direction, he pulled the family together and rounded up his herds and headed back towards his father's house. Since his previous behaviour had cost him the love of his brother Esau and replaced it with murderous intent, he soon discovered that his welcoming party consisted of 400 angry men committed, no doubt, to taking his life. Bad news travels fast and soon he learned that he was in a very undesirable place to meet an enemy. You could say he was between a rock and a hard place. There was no wall to protect him and no friends to defend him; he was completely at the mercy of what was coming. You can see him as he questions God, "Why would You give me these many blessings only to take them away from me? Why would You build me up to tear me down? Is this some sadistic game that You play to make me pay for my sinful actions?" He tried buying out his brother by sending gifts and flattery; he divided his family in hopes that at least part of it would survive. It was not until he found a place on the other side of Jabbok that he had his audience with God. It is not the kind of audience he expected but it did bring about the result that he desired even if there was a lingering consequence to remind him of this special encounter.

> *"That night Jacob got up and took his two wives, his two female servants and his eleven sons and crossed the ford of the Jabbok. [23] After he had sent them across the stream, he sent over all his possessions. [24] So Jacob was left alone, and a man wrestled with him till daybreak. [25] When the man saw that he could not overpower him, he touched the socket of Jacob's hip so that his hip was wrenched as he wrestled with the man. [26] Then the man said, "Let me go, for it is daybreak."*
>
> *But Jacob replied, "I will not let you go unless you bless me." [27] "The man asked him, "What is your name?" "Jacob," he answered."*
>
> *[28] "Then the man said, "Your name will no longer be Jacob, but Israel, because you have struggled with God and with humans and have overcome."*
>
> *[29] "Jacob said, "Please tell me your name." "But he replied, "Why do you ask my name?" Then he blessed him there." [30] "So Jacob called the place Peniel, saying, "It is because I saw God face to face,and yet my life was spared."*

> 31 *"The sun rose above him as he passed Peniel, and he was limping because of his hip.* 32 *Therefore to this day the Israelites do not eat the tendon attached to the socket of the hip, because the socket of Jacob's hip was touched near the tendon."* (Genesis 32: 22-32, NIV)

Now I do not know about you, but I find this very interesting. God bore a temporary body and met with Jacob in a very earthly manner. He wrestled with him; yes, I said God wrestled with Jacob. I am not sure if Jacob realized that God was allowing him to prevail and it was not because of his great strength. God was testing his resolve. How long are you willing to travail; how badly do you want a blessing? Notice how God gave him a chance to quit, "Let me go", He said. Jacob quickly answers, "I will not until you bless me." Certainly, I do not need to remind you that the One who created the heavens in one day certainly could overcome a middle-aged man in a wrestling match. What was His purpose then? For what reason would He do something He had never done before nor since: wrestle with a man? Or wait, has He? It's quite possible you may have wrestled with Him in travail over a situation that was overwhelming you, your prayers grabbing hold of God's arms and legs refusing to let go until He blessed you with an answer. Notice, he wrestled through the night and not the day. There is a principle there, for the scripture says:

> "*For His anger lasts only a moment, but His favor, a lifetime. Weeping may spend the night, but there is joy in the morning.*" (Psalm 30:5, HCSB)

In a previous book I focused on the topic "When the Dawn Breaks". In scripture darkness often represents struggle or the battle of evil. Light represents revelation and understanding. Jacob made it through the night, and may I say it was a very long night. Job, in like manner, made it through an extremely long night as well, but in the morning there was enlightenment and understanding. It may be, as you read these words that you are facing your own night of struggle. Maybe that's the reason you were attracted to this book. Let me tell you to not give up or let loose of the faith you are holding onto. Even though it's hard to hold onto, please make sure that you do, for the dawn is coming and blessings are waiting and understanding will meet you at the door of the sunrise.

It could quite possibly be said that Job had never experienced in his entire lifetime any experiences that could compare to these horrendous moments of grief and suffering. How do you prepare for moments like these? A young soldier can go through his basic training and even perform under live fire but nothing in his training prepares him for the horror of battle: the smells of sulfur, the cries of the dying, the chaos and confusion. Fear is gripping your heart but there is no place to hide and no direction to move but forward. How do you prepare for the first kill; how do you cope with the helplessness as you stand by the mortally wounded and hear their cries for help? There is an overwhelming hopelessness and shock that creeps into your mind which causes you to block out the scene.

As Job held the lifeless bodies of his children, he felt helpless, realizing death had stolen meaning from his life, leaving only a shell of what once was. He went from one child to another, remembering the happy family and hopes of yesterday that fled into the night and left him all alone. He looked to heaven and asked "Why?" and no answer came to soothe his pain or give guidance to his all-consuming grief. He was engulfed in the blackness of despair with no one to take him by the hand and refresh his focus. More than anything that has happened this day, this scene was the worst. Death and satan taunted him and showed him the weaknesses of mortality. God had turned and was now cultivating the soil of his life. What he was experiencing was allowing a broader spiritual dimension like an evening fog to envelop his conceptions of reality.

Pain and suffering drive away the things we value most and reveal dimensions that go beyond our perceived reality into a higher sensitivity of God and to the needs of those around us.

EXPERIENCE … THE ULTIMATE TEACHER

I often listen to young preachers just out of college who are on the road to establishing their own identity. They have acquired knowledge and now it is time to let experiences provide the foundation for wisdom. Oh, their messages are full of energy and eloquence but in most cases, lack the depth that comes from suffering. They tell of the suffering of others but have no venue from which to share their own. I often share with my hospice patients as I visit them in their homes that they will have four different types of people that will come to see them:

1. Those that bring cynicism, pointing out the reason for their suffering.
2. Those that bring sympathy.
3. Those that bring empathy.
4. Those few select groups who bring compassion.

In Job's case, there is evidence of the first group and that is the group that brings analysis and false hypotheses bordering on suspicion and a healthy serving of criticism.

Sympathy is the very least that you can bring to the table. It's like the guy who comes to a buffet with his wife and five kids and brings a bag of chips to pass.

Empathy brings experience that is similar, which allows the heart of the bearer to share in the feelings of the individual and provide hope.

Compassion, however, is the greatest gift of all; the word itself could be translated "to bear the suffering of others ". This is the person who holds you up when you cannot stand and prays in your place when you cannot even mouth the words. A compassionate person becomes a type of bridge that spans the gulf between hopelessness and leads to faith.

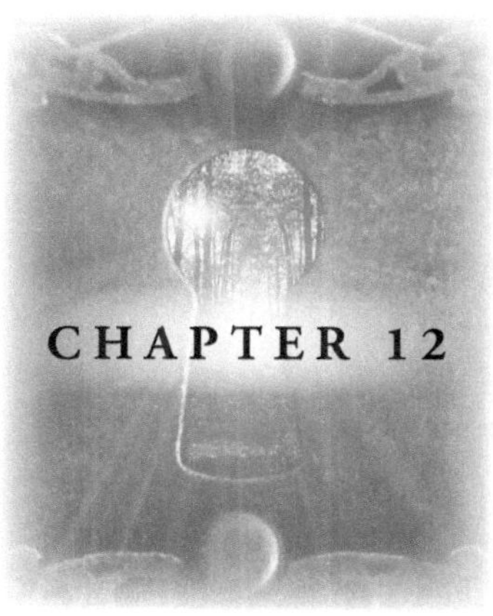

ANGELS DON'T ALWAYS HAVE WINGS

This last week I was at a church camp and ran into a friend I had not seen for quite some time. This person asked how I was doing. I mentioned that I had suffered an injury at work and had been recovering. Her questionable words of comfort were, "Oh, you always have something going on!" These words provided no comfort; they actually provided guilt. Is there something wrong with me? Am I a hypochondriac? Satan has a way of filling in the blanks in your thought process.

I remember several years ago, I went through a very difficult open-heart surgery. It was a surgery that had led to a number of complications. I did not know if I would make it. I had developed pneumonia right out of surgery and for the next five weeks I wrestled through every step of recovery. During this time my lungs kept filling with fluid which led to multiple thoracenteses. I can never remember a time in my life that I was so physically and spiritually depleted. I was struggling and almost past experiencing any emotion at all.

It was during one of the thoracenteses that I was approached by a physician who, by his sullen demeanor, could only be the bearer of bad news. I was waiting for one of my lungs to re-inflate after the procedure. I was also told they wanted to do an x-ray to make sure that they had completely drained all the fluid from my lungs. While I was waiting, my attending physician approached my bed and placed his hand on mine. I remember the moment as though it was yesterday. I remember praying, "Please God, no more! I cannot bear any more than what I have at this moment." I pleaded with Him to allow me to have time to recover from one calamity before I faced another. The doctor cleared his throat and looked at me with a sympathetic eye and said, "Steve, I know this is not a good time to share this information, but we feel that this discovery is significant enough that we need to address it as soon as possible." He went on to say that during their numerous scans they had come across an anomaly that they were quite concerned about on my spine. It was very suspicious and they felt that they needed to biopsy the mass they had discovered as soon as possible. That afternoon I remember feeling something breaking inside of me. It was like the snapping of a twig. I know some of you may not understand but I shut down emotionally. It was like I was living outside of my body. I felt like I was on a carousel spinning and spinning round and round and was no longer acclimated to where I was or where I was going. The biopsy was taken after some difficulty and turned out to be benign.

My dear wife stayed by my side each day and eventually I was able to pull myself up to a moderate state of self-reliance. I was back home at last. Then it happened: I had something go amiss in my heart and I was transported to a trauma center in Milwaukee and placed in intensive care. I was overcome with despair and slid into depression. "Please, I called out to God, have mercy!" I had no tears left. It was about two o'clock in the morning, one very long night, that I had feelings of giving up. I cannot express the depths of my despair as I pulled myself to the edge of the bed and forced myself into a sitting position. I was ready to throw in the towel. I know some of those who are reading this will relate to what I was feeling. I was weak, not only physically but spiritually.

It was then in the midst of this darkness that the door opened to my room and a nurse dressed in white came in. She silently came to where I was and asked if she could sit with me. She took my hand in hers and sat beside me. I felt her concern and compassion as she rubbed the back of my hand. I think she knew where I was, spiritually and physically. I felt a strength come into me that could only have come from God. She may have been an angel for she rarely said a word but just sat next to me. I remember such a warm and comforting presence. Then the words to a chorus filled my mind and the message that it brought opened the dam of emotion in my heart and the tears flowed like a summer squall. The song came from a Psalm of David.

> *"I will lift up mine eyes to the hills from whence cometh my help, [2] my help cometh from the Lord, the Lord who made heaven and earth, [3] He said he would not suffer my foot to be moved the Lord that healeth me, He will not slumber nor sleep, [5] oh the Lord is my shelter the Lord is my strength on my right hand [6] no the sun will not smite me by day nor the moon by night [7] he will restore my soul, My Help, My Help all of my help cometh from the Lord". (Psalms 121:1-7, KJV)*

It seemed like the room filled with a cloud of His presence and that through this lovely and sensitive nurse, God was holding my hand and reminding me of His nearness. This is just one of many such experiences where I have climbed out of the ashes of my struggle to go on to the High Places of God. After my recovery, I was determined to be to others what this nurse had been to me. I wanted to bring a comforting and calming presence to those, who like myself, were hurting.

I have found at times one's empathetic and loving presence can be much more effective than hollow words of sympathy.

CHAPTER 13

OVERCOMING PEOPLE'S GOOD INTENTIONS

Job at the moment longed for someone to provide him presence and spiritual strength so that he could go on. Satan had another card in his hand and now he was ready to put it on the table. The Bible calls those that now come to minister to Job, his "friends". I would have to say personally, with friends like those who needs enemies?

The greatest caregivers are the ones who have themselves, at one time or another, also needed care. They have fought the darkness of their own loss and suffering and go on to help others that are suffering.

Obviously, Job's four "friends" could not relate to Job. They brought their religiosity and piousness to the bedside of a broken man. They relished in the fact that they could look down on a man that they once had to look up to. They elevated themselves by standing on Job's shoulders.

They thought that the righteous should not suffer or endure pain. Like many today, they have all the answers as to why you are where you are. "God does not want you to go through this; you are here because of what you have done in secret. God is punishing you. Your faith is weak, for if you had strong faith you would not be where you are." These are coined answers to a complex spiritual construction. As we clearly see from hindsight as we read the Book of Job, they could not have been further from the truth. Job was exactly where God could use him the most. The struggles we read in the Book of Job have provided mountains of insight to people like Job that God knows their address and not only relates but delivers them from their pain.

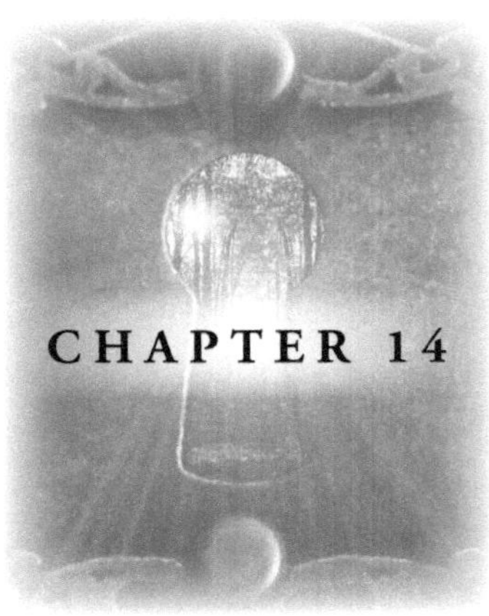

CHAPTER 14

A DREAM TO HOLD ONTO

One of my favorite characters in the Old Testament is a young man named Joseph. We met Joseph when he was just a teenager. Like most young people he had not developed a base of experience in life from which to draw wisdom.

God gave Joseph a promise of a future time in which his brethren would bow down to him as stated below in Genesis 37:

> *"And he dreamed yet another dream, and told it to his brethren, and said, Behold, I have dreamed a dream more; and, behold, the sun and the moon and the eleven stars made obeisance to me. [10] And he told it to his father, and his brethren: and his father rebuked him, and said unto him, What is this dream that thou hast dreamed? Shall I and thy mother and thy brethren indeed come to bow down ourselves to thee to the earth? [11] And his brethren envied him; but his father observed the saying." (Genesis 37:9-11, KJV)*

This promise represented authority and power through an elevated position in his life. However, he was not just promoted into this place in one day. He arrived at the position through the divine providence of God. He was 17 years old when he was sold into slavery. However, he was 30 years old when he was elevated to second in command under Pharaoh and the fulfillment of the dream took place. That was 13 years of waiting! First, he was cast down into a pit, then sold as a slave to a man named Potiphar and then cast into a prison for several years! Now, from a point of casual observation, it looked like Joseph was headed in the wrong direction. He lost everything before he gained God's promise. What was God thinking?

However, Joseph was exactly where God wanted him to be. He was learning the traits of a good and godly leader. He held onto his faith and it grew; he held on to his integrity and that also grew. He learned empathy and compassion for others who were accused falsely and thrown into unfair treatment. Couldn't God just have elevated him right away to this position without the pit, servanthood and the prison? Yes, He could have, but would Joseph have been the type of leader he was without the experience he gained?

I remember a story about a little boy who happened to find a cocoon while playing outside. He brought it to his parents and they explained to him what was taking place in the cocoon, how the little caterpillar was in the process of becoming a beautiful butterfly. They placed the cocoon above the fireplace in their living room and each day the little boy would walk by and look at it. One day however, as he passed by, he noticed that the cocoon was shaking and he thought about the poor caterpillar inside and how he must be longing to get out of that dreadful place. So he took the cocoon down and opened it up to release this little creature.

Sure enough, inside was a beautiful butterfly! He placed the butterfly on the mantle but it could not fly and eventually died. This troubled the little boy and he asked his father why the butterfly died. His father placed his hand on the shoulder of his troubled son and said, "When you saw the cocoon shaking, what was happening inside was that this little butterfly was developing strength so when the day came that it was time to get out he would have the ability to fly. When you released him from the cocoon he never had the time to completely develop and could not survive. You see, struggles make us stronger and allow us to survive the elements of resistance that enter into our lives." In other words, many times those things that we think are hurting us are the same things that are making us stronger.

When Joseph was elevated to his high position in Egypt, his brothers who had sold him into slavery were very concerned about what Joseph might do to them. Joseph, however, in his wisdom understood how God had used divine providence to bring about these events in his life. Although his experiences were long and hard, the effects would be long-lasting and provide a place of safety and provision during, not only a future famine, but for the birth of a nation.

> "*Then his brothers also went and fell down before his face, and they said, "Behold, we are your servants."* [19] *Joseph said to them, "Do not be afraid, for am I in the place of God?* [20] *But as for you, you meant evil against me; but God meant it for good, in order to bring it about as it is this day, to save many people alive.* [21] *Now therefore, do not be afraid; I will provide for you and your little ones.*" (Genesis 50:18-21, KJV)

There were three major events that tried to sap the vision away that God had shared with Joseph: The Pit, Potiphar, and the Prison. What was it that kept Joseph going? I truly believe that he rehearsed that dream over and over again in his mind. He reminded himself that God does not lie and that He is faithful to His promises. Just as Abraham laid Isaac on the altar, he rehearsed the promise that God had given him that his seed would multiply and not cease to exist.

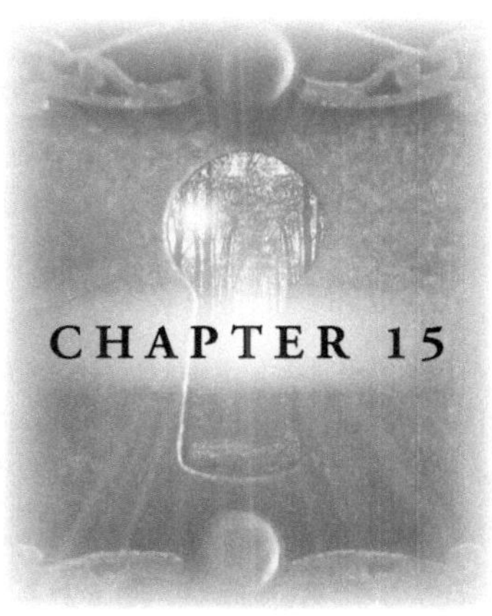

HOPE ... THE FORERUNNER OF FAITH

One of the Fruit of the Spirit is Hope. When we lose hope we lose purpose and without purpose we lose direction. Paul said it so well in the Book of Romans:

> *"For we are saved by hope: but hope that is seen is not hope: for what a man seeth, why doth he yet hope for?* [25] *But if we hope for that we see not, then do we with patience wait for it."* (Romans 8:24-25, KJV)

Have you ever misplaced your hope? Has your faith ever been buried under the circumstances and disillusionment that comes via the venue of pain and suffering? Have you ever been thrown into a pit of despair and charged with an action that was maliciously formed to hurt and destroy you? Have you been locked in a situation that takes away your liberty to grow and live a normal life?

Joseph, like Job, is a living memorial testifying that God does not forsake His own. He never promised us that there would be no pain; He never promised that every day would be a paradise. However, He did promise that He would never leave us nor forsake us.

> *"The Lord was with Joseph, and he was a successful man; and he was in the house of his master the Egyptian. [3] And his master saw that the Lord was with him and that the Lord made all he did to prosper in his hand."* (Genesis 39: 2-3, KJV)

> *"So Joseph's master took him and had him thrown into the prison where the king's prisoners were confined. While Joseph was there in the prison, [21] the LORD was with him and extended kindness to him. He granted him favor in the eyes of the prison warden, [22] who put all those held in the prison under Joseph's authority, so that he was responsible for all that was done there."* (Genesis 39:20-22, NIV)

The Lord blessed Joseph in spite of his circumstances. Not only did Joseph learn humility but God was creating a vessel that would save His people from impending tragedy. Pharoah tapped into the knowledge and Spirit that dwelt in Joseph to save his own nation after he was warned by God in a dream of a great dearth that was about to face the land.

Now we all could have hoped that Joseph would not have had to go through the things that he did but how would that have affected the untold nations that were spared death because of his suffering and loss? There's a popular saying I hear frequently, "It's not all about you." Many of us may think that it is, but in the end our lives affect countless people and the things that we experience bring us not only added strength and trust in God's promises, but they lead us to our mission field of labor.

If we endure the fiery trials we face, they will purify us; if we surrender to the trial, it will destroy us.

> *"In all this you greatly rejoice, though now for a little while you may have had to suffer grief in all kinds of trials.* [7] *These have come so that the proven genuineness of your faith—of greater worth than gold, which perishes even though refined by fire—may result in praise, glory and honor when Jesus Christ is revealed."* (1 Peter 1:6-7, NIV)

If we can understand that there is a purpose in the valley that we are walking through, we will not be tempted to turn back or give up.

We are all familiar with the Ten Commandments given to Moses on Mount Sinai. They were a moral key to intimacy with God. Many of these commandments are emblazoned in the center of man's conscience. Do not kill, do not steal, do not commit adultery and they establish a premise for a spiritual relationship with a sinless God. However, when we enter into the New Testament, Jesus goes through nine traits that every Christian should strive to live by in addition to the law given to Moses.

The Beatitudes:

"The poor in spirit are blessed, for the kingdom of heaven is theirs.
[4] *Those who mourn are blessed, for they will be comforted.*
[5] *The gentle are blessed, for they will inherit the earth.*
[6] *Those who hunger and thirst for righteousness are blessed, for they will be filled.*
[7] *The merciful are blessed, for they will be shown mercy.*
[8] *The pure in heart are blessed, for they will see God.*
[9] *The peacemakers are blessed, for they will be called sons of God.*
[10] *Those who are persecuted for righteousness are blessed, for the kingdom of heaven is theirs.*
[11] *"You are blessed when they insult and persecute you and falsely say every kind of evil against you because of Me.* [12] *Be glad and rejoice, because your reward is great in heaven. For that is how they persecuted the prophets who were before you."* (Matthew 5:3-12, HSB)

In a number of these blessings it would not be uncommon for someone to feel anything but blessed. How about the person who is mourning? Does he feel blessed? How about those persecuted for righteousness sake? That is not a common or an immediate feeling that normally pops up. How about when people persecute you and lie about you and say all manner of evil against you? The Lord speaks out to those and says, "*Rejoice and be glad for your reward is great in heaven.*" (Matthew 5:12, NIV)

See, we need to understand that as Christians we have a dual spirit; we have our carnal spirit that likes to live in the here and now and seeks immediate gratification for its desires. But as a Christian filled with God's Spirit, we have another nature that responds not just to the present but focuses on future outcomes as well. It does this because it is an eternal spirit. This eternal spirit sees things from a completely different perspective than that of our carnal spirit. It values a humble spirit for it knows that a humble spirit leads to the inheritance of God. For instance, God speaks to Israel as follows:

> "*If my people, which are called by my name, shall humble themselves, pray and seek my face and turn from their wicked ways, then I will hear from heaven, and will heal their land.*" (2 Chronicles 7:14, NIV)

God is drawn to the humble and contrite spirit of His children.

> "*For this is what the high and exalted One says— he who lives forever, whose name is holy: "I live in a high and holy place, but also with the one who is contrite and lowly in spirit, to revive the spirit of the lowly and to revive the heart of the contrite.*" (Isaiah 57:15, NIV)

Years ago, I remember the first time I read in the Book of Acts, the account of the disciples how they were chastised and beaten for continuing to preach after they were instructed to stop. Their response surprised me because it did not make sense to me at that time. Many of these disciples were present at the Sermon on the Mount and they remembered the words of Christ concerning persecution and false accusation. Look how they responded:

> "*At this, they yielded to Gamaliel. They called the apostles in and had them flogged. Then they ordered them not to speak in the name of Jesus, and released them.* [41] *The apostles left the Sanhedrin, rejoicing that they had been counted worthy of suffering disgrace for the Name.* [42] *Every day, in the temple courts and from house to house, they did not stop teaching and proclaiming the good news that Jesus is the Christ....*" (Acts 5:40-42, NIV)

Let me ask this question: Does it sound like they grasped the principles of the Beatitudes? Did they understand that blessings come through struggle and pain and can sometimes lead to exaltation? Do we feel this way when similar things happen? We do when we change our focus and start looking at our situation through the image of the Cross and not through the pain of our struggles.

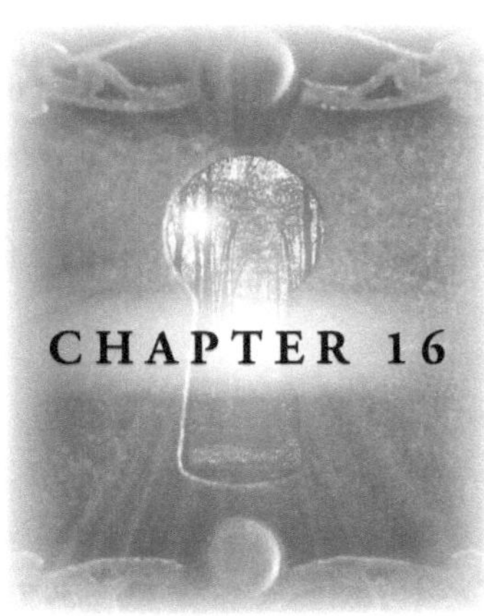

CHAPTER 16

A ROAD OF SUFFERING IS THE QUICKEST ROUTE TO EMPATHY

Remember what Joseph told his brothers when they feared his retribution for their acts of deceit and vengeance in Genesis 50:

> *"Joseph said to them, "Do not be afraid, for am I in the place of God? 20 But as for you, you meant evil against me; but God meant it for good, in order to bring it about as it is this day, to save many people alive."* (Genesis 50:19-20, NKJV)

Notice the last part of the verse; not only did the calamities and suffering he faced benefit him in the end but it preserved the lives of many people. It's time for us to understand that the troubles we face are just for a season; the fruit produced by suffering endures forever.

Some time ago I had my gallbladder removed. I had some anxiety about this procedure because my Uncle Donald died after having his removed due to complications. My procedure went well. Later, in the recovery room, I was told I needed to use the restroom before they could release me - not a bad idea knowing my bladder! While I was in the restroom, I had a terrible pain in my head and I called out for help. I thought for sure I was going to pass out! They rushed me to the emergency room and then sent me in for an MRI. After the images were interpreted, I was informed that I had a mass in my brain and that I needed to seek assistance promptly to have this addressed.

Therefore I went to the Chief Surgeon of Neurology at St Luke's Hospital in Milwaukee. He was said to be the best Neurologist there was in our area. He showed me the mass and then described his plan to remove it. It involved cutting into my skull and I was told I would, no doubt, have seizures for a time after the surgery. I do not have to tell you the fear that I was experiencing.

I was pastoring at the time and of course, pastors never wrestle with things like anxiety because they have special abilities that no one else has. Don't believe that for a second! Anyone who lives in a human body will have human emotions and fears, however, I hid mine from the members of our church. I didn't even want to tell my pastor friends what I was going through because I just knew Job's friends would show up and try to figure out why all these things were happening to me. I prayed to God and tried to trust in His direction as best as I could, but I knew that I was living in denial. We need each other to encourage and exhort one another in the midst of struggle. It just so happened that we had a ministerial conference near the city where I live. I had a district duty at the event which involved spending time away from the sanctuary and being more in a service capacity than a leadership capacity.

My brother Rick was one of the few people I let know about what was going on and I swore him to secrecy. Unfortunately, or maybe I should say fortunately, he shared the news with another minister who shared it with another one and you know where it went from there. At this conference I was summoned into the sanctuary and brought up to the front. The thing I feared most was about to happen. They were going to make me focus on this situation and acknowledge that I needed help from above. My fellow pastors were all informed of my situation and the possible ramifications. I felt a whole lot of sympathetic eyes drilling through the back of my head. I know they all loved me; I knew they were concerned about me, but what I feared most in my flesh happened. After the prayer of this wonderful congregation, everyone that talked to me made me feel like they were saying goodbye. They had great intentions but I really needed a little empathy and a lot of compassion as we talked about earlier in this book. I had resigned myself to God's will whatever that might be.

I was scheduled for one more radiology exam before the surgery was to take place to have them confirm their plan for surgery. I will never forget what happened in that Surgeon's office as my family gathered around. The Surgeon became upset and quickly grabbed his phone and called radiology for the mass was gone and could not be seen! I have to be honest; I saw a great big smile come across Rick's face and I wanted to rejoice at that moment but held back. Really? It's gone, you mean like it's not there? Did it move somewhere else?

Your human reasoning can be so humorous at times as we are afraid to grasp hold of a miracle. Or, is it that we're afraid to be picked up out of our despondency only to be dropped back in when our hope is crashed again? It was gone and that was that! I realized that night as all the ministers prayed, God did His own major surgery on my brain without me even knowing. That, my friend, is the kind of surgery that I like best. I happened to be working at the hospital where it was first diagnosed and knew the Radiologist who first read the initial report. I asked if I could meet with him for a little while. I shared with him what had happened and he quickly brought up the pictures on his screen. I asked him what he thought and he very clearly told me that there was no doubt that the diagnosis was accurate and that I should be extremely happy for it was no longer there.

In a sense I felt like one of the three Hebrew children who were cast into the fire of Nebuchadnezzar's furnace but instead of being consumed by the flames I found that God was waiting there for my arrival and had everything under control. What could have killed me only fired up my faith and provided fuel to the power of God's intercession.

How come God does not do that every time? What about my heart condition and heart surgery? What about the many times that I cried out and felt that I was not delivered from my situation? Why is God not consistent and why does He not do that all the time? Well, let me put it this way. If you have a child, can you remember when he or she first started to walk and they fell down and hit their head on the coffee table? Boy, doesn't that seem to happen to everyone's kid at one time or another? Do you remember rushing over and picking him or her up and holding them and comforting them? Putting a little ice cube on the bump on their head? I ask you this question: "Was that the last time they fell?" Of course not; you picked them up for a while but eventually they learned to get up themselves and eventually learned to respect the corner of the coffee table. Sometimes God picks us up and heals us, but other times He allows us to walk through our pain. How often have I heard someone say to someone else that got hurt during an activity, to just walk it off? Sometimes God wants me to walk it off, for these trials of life toughen up our character and make us more watchful of our actions. It also, and most importantly, allows us to share in other people's pain and provide the compassion that helps them through their trial.

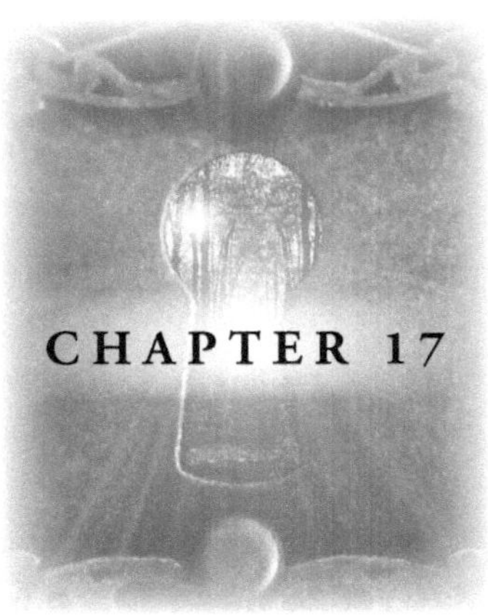

CHAPTER 17

EQUIPPED FOR STRUGGLE ... BORN FOR ADVERSITY

In 1999 Lisa and I both felt the Lord leading us into another field of labor. We had been pastoring in the Sheboygan Falls area in Wisconsin for a number of years. It was so hard to say goodbye to the members who we dearly loved with all of our heart. The pull of God to make this change was overwhelming.

So, like the Clampetts in the Beverly Hillbillies we loaded up the truck, literally, and moved to Eagle, WI.

We both felt strongly that God was directing us to Abundant Life Apostolic Church in Oconomowoc, WI where I would become Associate Pastor. I mention emphatically that both my wife and I felt strongly that this is what God wanted us to do; we had prayed and sought God about this change for quite some time. For those first four years things went well for our family. Now some who are going to read this may feel what I am about to say is quite absurd. However, I must remind you that God, in His Word, specifically tells us in the last days these words:

> *"And afterward, I will pour out My Spirit on all people. Your sons and daughters will prophesy, your old men will dream dreams,your young men will see visions.* [29] *Even on My menservants and maidservants, I will pour out My Spirit in those days. . . .*" (Joel 2:28-29, NIV)

Now saying that, I share with you this experience. It was a summer afternoon; I had walked the 300-foot long trek to our mailbox and was returning back to the house. Somewhere along the way, God interrupted my walk and gave me a vision. I remained on the driveway but now, instead of clear skies I saw a storm approaching; the clouds were black as night and rolling and churning. This happened so quickly that my heart went to my throat and I realized that I must make it to the house before I am swept up in this terrible storm. In this vision, I began to run as fast as I could but realized that there was no way that I was going to make it to shelter before I would be engulfed in the blackness and fury of the storm.

Just as the storm reached me, I found that I was above it; that's right, I was sustained above the clouds and was looking down upon the storm, safely protected from its fury. After some time as I was gazing at the earth, my eyes fell upon an animal of some kind. I felt directed to speak to the animal words of death and of life. I realized that with my voice I had power to cause life or death. I found myself shortly afterward, standing by myself and a voice asked me this question: "What gift is it that you desire?" Now I do not know about you but there are a lot of things that I could ask God for. I understood that He was asking me to petition Him for anything I desired. The words that came forth from my mouth surprised me because I asked God for the ability to walk through walls. God granted that gift. I was standing near a wall and I purposed to try this gift. I pressed against the wall and it seemed nothing happened. I pushed with all my strength and then I realized I was able to pass through this barrier even though it took perseverance.

Immediately afterward I was back in my driveway. At that point in my life, little did I know that a huge storm was heading into our family's life. I had no idea what was ahead but eventually the storm of life hit me like a ton of bricks. It was this vision that helped to sustain me through the weeks and months ahead as my world changed. At times I did not know how I was going to make it through but God was allowing me to walk through the wall of resistance that surrounded me. God carried me above the storm and instead of it destroying me it did quite the opposite. I was able to see the storm from a different perspective that provided spiritual empowerment. Job, in a similar way, had no idea the fierceness of the trial that was sweeping down upon his perfect little world. His roots were buried deep in God's promises and though the tree was bent to the point of breaking, it held firm.

Those things that sweep into our lives unexpectedly test our stability and root system. If I am a day-by-day Christian, one who lives moment-to-moment, and is affected by every current of adversity, my life will become unsteady and my boat may come close to capsizing. However, each time I overcome adversity, my boat becomes a little more stable. My sail becomes a little bit wider and my rudder more versatile.

The Bible is full of examples such as these, men and women just like you and me, people that loved God and often endured circumstances that enlarged their perspective of God. I have noticed that the sweetest spirits are usually born out of the most bitter of circumstances.

JESUS ... THE ONE WHOM YOU LOVE IS SICK

There is a little Town near Jerusalem called Bethany. It is the home of three very precious individuals: Lazarus and his two sisters, Mary and Martha. A more wonderful and hospitable family would be hard to find. It's understandable why Jesus spent so much time in this home with His disciples.

> "*Now Jesus loved Martha and her sister and Lazarus*" (John 11:5, NIV)

These four had a very special relationship. There was laughter as well as an openness in their times together. The three of them felt security and privilege in His presence. This man was the Healer, the hope of mankind, and in His presence they sensed the awesomeness of God robed in a body. This, however, became part of the challenge they faced as Lazarus became very sick and Jesus was nowhere near to come and provide what He had done for countless others: His healing touch. The longer Jesus delayed in coming, the greater the struggle in their arena of faith. He was not there to hold Lazarus' hand or to increase their faith through His words of hope. We are not certain how long Lazarus was sick, or how long it took for the disease in his body to take the final flicker of his life.

No doubt the long nights that the sisters spent at their brother's side as they watched him fight to survive left scars on their relationship with Jesus. They trusted Him to come; they were told that their messages had been delivered and yet He chose not to come. What He had done for so many others would He not do for them, the ones whom He loved? I remind you of a previous statement I made: "Do we think it was easy for God to watch Job's trial and not interfere?" It was very hard to hold off, but the lesson that was being imparted was so much more valuable at that time than His intercession.

Job's role became a memorial of faith for countless others like ourselves who would find unexplained struggle in our own lives. In a similar manner, Mary and Martha could not see the enormous implications for those who would take up their own crosses in their march to the New Jerusalem. They saw the pain, they saw the suffering. They felt the emotions of hopelessness. Little did they know that there was a plan in place and Lazarus would play a great part in the drama that was unfolding, for the time was drawing near for Jesus' arrest and His time of suffering and death.

> *"Now a man named Lazarus was sick. He was from Bethany, the village of Mary and her sister Martha. [2] (This Mary, whose brother Lazarus now lay sick, was the same one who poured perfume on the Lord and wiped his feet with her hair.) [3] "So the sisters sent word to Jesus, "Lord, the one you love is sick."*
>
> *[4] When he heard this, Jesus said, "This sickness will not end in death. No, it is for God's glory so that God's Son may be glorified through it." [5] Now Jesus loved Martha and her sister and Lazarus. [6] So when he heard that Lazarus was sick, he stayed where he was two more days,"* (John 11:1-6, NIV)

Notice how the sisters address Jesus with their message, "*Lord the one you love.*" They are reminding Him of his own words. What others would not do because of inconvenience, they would do for love. *Jesus, they are indiscriminately saying, "If you love Lazarus, we know You will come.*" Is it possible the question in their mind had arisen that, "If God loves my brother, why is He not here ministering His healing touch?" Have you ever had that question pop into your mind? Have you ever questioned the depth of God's commitment to you when you were wrestling with the demons of fear and pain? We see this more clearly portrayed when Jesus does arrive in Bethany at the home of Mary and Martha and the now-deceased Lazarus.

> "*On his arrival, Jesus found that Lazarus had already been in the tomb for four days.* [18] *Now Bethany was less than two miles from Jerusalem,* [19] *and many Jews had come to Martha and Mary to comfort them in the loss of their brother.* [20] *When Martha heard that Jesus was coming, she went out to meet him, but Mary stayed at home.* [21] *"Lord," Martha said to Jesus, "if you had been here, my brother would not have died.* [22] *But I know that even now God will give you whatever you ask."* [23] *Jesus said to her, "Your brother will rise again."* [24] *Martha answered, "I know he will rise again in the resurrection at the last day.*" (John 11:17-24, NIV)

Martha leaves the house immediately; Mary stays at home. Do I sense some bitterness there, some feelings of disappointment? Look carefully at the first words that come forth from the mouth of Mary, "*If you had been here, my brother would not have died.*" Lord, you could have stopped this from happening. She was making Him accountable, not for what He did but for what He did not do. She had not totally given up even though she did not understand why. Mary's statement to Jesus carries in it a thread of hope covered with a sprinkling of doubt. "God will grant whatever you ask." This is one of those fluff statements that we make: "I know that God can do all things" - even though at this moment my barrel is empty and my jar of oil is nearly depleted. Jesus, at this point, offers hope, "*Your brother will rise again.*" But the mistrust has now taken hold and fear has clouded her window of faith and she mentions quite abruptly, "I know that; what good does that do me now? My brother is gone, my life is shattered and my joy and hope have crashed into the depths of despair!" I find it very intriguing how Jesus deals with this statement.

> *"Jesus said to her, "I am the resurrection and the life. The one who believes in me will live, even though they die;* [26] *and whoever lives by believing in me will never die. Do you believe this?"* [27] *"Yes, Lord," she replied, "I believe that you are the Messiah, the Son of God, who is to come into the world."* (John 11:25-27, NIV)

Jesus refers to Himself as the Resurrection. "Mary, do you know who I am? Do you understand that a person who believes in Me will never die?" Then He asks her a very important question. It's the same question I am going to ask you. You have read the scriptures, you have heard the claims, but do you believe this? Do you truly believe the promises that have been given or are you going to dodge the question like Martha does? "Yes, Lord, I believe that You are the Messiah, the Son of God."

Mary and Martha both come to grips with Jesus' statement that not only is Jesus a healer but he is the Resurrection. Hope does not cease when the body breathes its last breath. You both have a dead brother lying in a tomb not too far from where we are standing. Do you believe that I can raise him up?" Both Mary and Martha find themselves in the same predicament that another gentleman did when Jesus mentioned that he must believe. Look how he answers:

> *"Jesus said to him, "If you can believe, all things are possible to him who believes."* [24] *Immediately the father of the child cried out and said with tears, "Lord, I believe; help my unbelief!"* (Mark 9:23-24, NKJV)

You see God, I really do want to believe but right now my unbelief is making a lot more noise in the chambers of my faith than my trust and belief. This was a much more open and honest answer.

Martha ran back to get Mary and when she was persuaded to leave the house of doubt and come to Christ, the first words that came from her lips were identical to the words of her sister Martha. Do not think for one moment that these two sisters hadn't been talking about how Jesus had let them all down in not coming soon enough to heal their brother.

> "*When Mary reached the place where Jesus was and saw him, she fell at his feet and said, "Lord, if you had been here, my brother would not have died."* [33] *When Jesus saw her weeping, and the Jews who had come along with her also weeping, he was deeply moved in spirit and troubled.*" (John 11:32-33, NIV)

Is Jesus troubled by their tears? I truly believe He is more troubled by their lack of trust and faith. Could you have spent all this time with Him and never known Him? Could you have been a Christian all these years faithfully serving Him and in fellowship with Him and never really got to know Him? Jesus rebukes Phillip when he says these words in John 14:9:

> "*Jesus saith unto him, Have I been so long time with you, and yet hast thou not known me, Philip? he that hath seen me hath seen the Father; and how sayest thou then, Show us the Father?*"

We can have that kind of casual relationship in lives of mediocrity but it is in suffering and struggle we really get to know Him. Look what the Apostle Paul says:

> "*That I may know him, and the power of his resurrection, and the fellowship of his sufferings, being made conformable unto his death*"; (Philippians 3:10, KJV)

Notice how Paul mentions the fellowship of His suffering. Do you realize that a bond is developed in suffering? David states in Psalm 23:4, "*Yea, though I walk through the valley of the shadow of death, I shall fear no evil: for thou art with me; Your rod and Your staff, they comfort me*".

The day that Jesus stood outside the tomb of Lazarus, the scripture records this response: "*Jesus wept.*" (John 11:35, KJV) This is the shortest verse in the Bible; it contains two short words but no two words have ever been recorded that carried more meaning. Jesus wept. Did He weep because Lazarus whom He loved was dead? No, He did not. He wept at the unbelief of those He had invested His ministry in because, after all this time, they still did not believe He was whom He said He was. The Lord at this point does something that is not only prophetic of His own soon-coming death but also of every "born again" Christian who has ever lived. He calls out, "*Lazarus come forth.*" (John 11:43, KJV) Someone mentioned to me that it is a good thing He used Lazarus's name, otherwise everyone who had ever died would have responded to those words and exited tombs from around the world. In just a few days Jesus Himself was going to be in a tomb not so much unlike this tomb. He was going to be in the grave three days and three nights.

By this special act of resurrection he instilled hope for those who one day in the near future would be standing outside of His tomb wondering if earth's hope had died. He showed indisputable proof that He had power over a person who had already been dead four days. At Lazarus's resurrection, great faith was breathed into the heart of those believers. Lazarus lived again and went back home with his sisters but people that day went home with the visual picture of Christ's power over death. Yes, it was a very hard thing for Mary, Martha and Lazarus to go through but the fruit of their suffering has sustained millions upon millions over the years by the fact that God is able to restore that which is lost and replenish it more plentifully.

CHAPTER 19

GOD'S PURPOSES TRUMP OUR OWN

One of the most quoted scriptures in relationship to suffering is found in Romans 8:28:

> *"And we know that all things work together for good to those who love God, to those who are the called according to His purpose."*

When I look at this verse, two words seem to stick out more than the others. The first word is "things". This word is inclusive of all the stuff you may find yourself dealing with at any particular moment, the good "stuff" as well as the "not so desirable stuff". Now we know how the good stuff helps our life, like a job promotion or an increase in salary. It's easy for us to see the benefits in the acquiring side of our life, however, it is not so easy for us to understand the loss side in the spreadsheet of our daily lives. I find it really easy to thank God for the many blessings that flow into my life each day. Nevertheless, when the bucket of prosperity and pleasure springs a leak and the good seems to drain, it is much harder to deal with. Now the Bible wants us to grow accustomed to dealing not only with the acquisition of blessings but also with the loss of those things we consider valuable to our existence.

> *"In every thing give thanks: for this is the will of God in Christ Jesus concerning you.* [19] *Quench not the Spirit.* [20] *Despise not prophesyings.* [21] *Prove all things; hold fast that which is good.* [22] *Abstain from all appearance of evil."* (1 Thessalonians 5:18-22, KJV)

Paul again uses the word translated "thing" just as he did to the church in Rome. This means that we should constantly give thanks no matter what we are dealing with in our life at any particular moment. I know that it is hard to be thankful for a bad day when everything seems to go wrong. It's then we must go back and look at Romans 8 for Paul points out that whether we receive good from the Lord or not so good, they all work toward a purpose in our lives. Now let me point out, the purpose you may have in mind might be quite different from the purpose that God has in store. If our lives are full of flowers and rainbows every day and there are no cold dark nights with very little, if any discomfort, how could we appreciate the true blessings of God's goodness? How could we really enjoy a sunrise without the coming of the dawn? How could we truly appreciate our health if we never knew sickness or pain? The Bible mentions again that all things work together for good to those who love God and who are "the called" according to His purpose. Our lives are deeply intertwined with many others. God's purpose is to address the whole body of believers.

Let's look at an example: At this moment as I write, the sky is clear and it's a beautiful summer morning. However, on the other side of the world people who love God just as I do are experiencing the blackness of the night. We recognize the solar calendar, the seasons, and the fickleness of the weather. We think it is not strange to have subzero weather in the winter and oppressing heat in the summer. We should also understand that in our lives there are seasons. Solomon understood that when he wrote these words:

> "*To every thing there is a season, and a time to every purpose under the heaven:* [2] *A time to be born, and a time to die; a time to plant, and a time to pluck up that which is planted;* [3] *A time to kill, and a time to heal; a time to break down, and a time to build up;* [4] *A time to weep, and a time to laugh; a time to mourn, and a time to dance;*" (Ecclesiastes 3:1-4, KJV)

Job was suffering from the loss of many of those things he had once treasured. He lost his wealth, his children, his health and the respect of his peers. Then his wife, the woman closest to his heart, even turned against him and told him to give up and die and added while you're at it, curse God on your way out. Job answers her quite profoundly with these words:

> "*But he said unto her, "Thou speakest as one of the foolish women speaketh. What? Shall we receive good at the hand of God, and shall we not receive evil?" In all this did not Job sin with his lips.*" (Job 2:10, KJV)

I have learned that in my life there are seasons of harvest in which things are replenished and are fresh each day. I have also learned there are seasons in my life where I fight to maintain a positive perspective.

Life can be fickle and I find myself looking at the scars that cover my heart, each scar representing a hurt or loss that took time to heal. Now those scars can do one of two things: 1) they can encourage me as I look at each victorious battle or, 2) they can discourage me as I look at every struggle and the physical and emotional pain I had to suffer through. Only I can make that decision to control my thoughts and emotions.

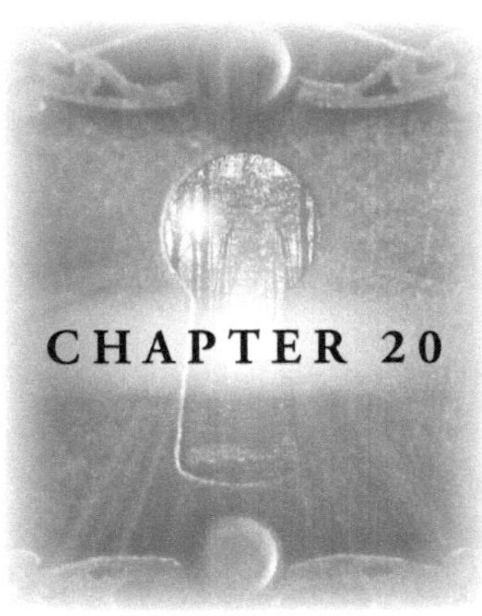

A PLACE OF SAFETY IN A TIME OF TORMENT AND PAIN

In the Old Testament the Bible tells us that Joshua was commanded by God to establish six cities of refuge: three were to be on the east side of Jordan and three were to be on the west side of Jordan. These cities were strategically positioned in such a way that those who needed to take advantage of their safety were always close to a haven of refuge. They were placed for those who accidentally were involved in the death of another person. You see, it was the right of the deceased's near kinsman to take vengeance upon the person responsible for the death of his near relative, accidental or not. Needless to say, the person responsible for the death expedited his arrival to the city of refuge closest to him lest the near kinsman meet him on the way and take his life. Now I am not insinuating even in a remote way that you, my friend, are guilty of such a thing but I wholeheartedly believe that God has a place of refuge close to His people where they may flee from guilt and unrelenting pain. It's a place of peace and safety where the things that haunt us are kept at bay.

Most of us are aware of Proverbs 18:10 which states, "*the Name of the Lord is a strong tower: the righteous runneth into it and is safe*". I remember a time many years ago; I was about 19 at the time. I had made several life-changing mistakes and oh, how they haunted me! My guilt was overwhelming, my hope depleted and I had reached a point in which I wondered if I could continue to face another day. I was looking for hope; I was looking for peace and a place of refuge. I needed more than a friend, I needed more than nice consoling words, I needed strong arms and a place of renewal.

It was late one Friday night that I stumbled into a dark, empty church building. I made my way quickly to the front of the sanctuary and fell, exhausted, on my knees. My voice cracked with emotion as I called out to the only One that knew my heart and circumstances! It was there in the dark that the light shone upon my heart and the warmth and compassion of God's love surrounded me. I received the gift of hope that night. I received hope and God's protective hands drove off the demons of failure which chased me as I entered into the loving arms of God.

Now I do not know what circumstances led you to pick up this book and I guess it is not really important that I do. However, I know whatever circumstance you find yourself in, that there is a place of refuge near enough for you to reach. There is a God in heaven who holds the door open for you as you expend the last remnants of your strength crossing the threshold of grace. No doubt He has left the light on for you to find your way in the dark.

In Luke 15:11-32 we have the Parable of the Prodigal Son. We have two sons, one who was content to serve his father and wait for the blessing of the inheritance which one day would be his. The other was discontented and restless and foolishly took an early inheritance and squandered it on things that only temporarily seemed to satisfy. His decisions lead him to spiritual and financial depravity. His emotional state was nearly at the bottom of the scope of hope. The only way for him to survive another day was to find employment with a person who raised pigs, something no good Jew would ever touch or eat for it was an unclean animal. I guess when you are desperate there are no limits to what you will do to survive. Talk about a shot to his self-image, from the mansion of his father's estate to the squander of a peasant's pig pen. He found himself envying the food that the pigs ate. It was in the mire of this existence that the miracle of transformation took place. It was here where the caterpillar began to change into the butterfly it was meant to be.

God allows us to make our own decisions and sometimes, in the case of the prodigal, they bring us to the pits of spiritual and emotional poverty. Where was the boy's father; did he care that his son was suffering through this ordeal? The father realized that struggle and despair can benefit us more than prosperity and blessing. Don't believe for a second that he was not watching the road each day hoping for the return of his son, a son who had squandered what the father had worked so hard for. The Bible states that the young man came onto himself one day and a light turned on in his mind and he was able to see what surrounded him and the man he had become. Remorse streamed into his heart as he saw himself through his father's eyes. Remorse and repentance always stimulate spiritual movement and growth. I think that is why Joseph, in the Book of Genesis, is recorded as saying, "*As for you, you meant evil against me, but God meant it for good.*" The same hammer that can crack a walnut is able to build a home.

The "key" is leaving the area of your torment and relocating to a place of provision and protection. I am not talking about a location or locality; I am talking about a spiritual place where the righteous can run to and be safe. It is nearer than you think to where you are. That young man, as he walked toward his father's house, no doubt wondered what kind of a reception he would receive. However, the scripture mentions that the father saw him at a great distance and ran to meet him and embraced him and put a ring on his finger and a new robe upon his shoulders. He also placed sandals upon his feet. One who was lost and destitute, who had no one that cared or watched for his soul, had once again entered into the realm of his father's protection and sustenance. That night he ate from the best of the herd and sat around the master's fire. For he had once been lost but now was home and the whole house rejoiced at his homecoming!

ARE YOU A PRISONER OF CHRIST OR A PRISONER OF YOUR SITUATION?

It is believed this letter to the Philippians was written in 62 AD. Paul was supposedly martyred after the great fire in Rome in July of 64 AD. So Paul wrote this two years before his death. Paul is in custody when he writes this letter as well as the letters to the Colossians, Ephesians and Philemon. All four are prison Epistles.

> *"Paul and Timothy, servants of Christ Jesus,*
> *To all God's holy people in Christ Jesus at Philippi,*
> *together with the overseers and deacons:* [2] *Grace and*
> *peace to you from God our Father and the Lord Jesus*
> *Christ.* [3] *I thank my God every time I remember you.*
> [4] *In all my prayers for all of you, I always pray with*
> *joy* [5] *because of your partnership in the gospel from*
> *the first day until now,* [6] *being confident of this, that*

he who began a good work in you will carry it on to completion until the day of Christ Jesus.

[7] *It is right for me to feel this way about all of you, since I have you in my heart and, whether I am in chains or defending and confirming the gospel, all of you share in God's grace with me.* [8] *God can testify how I long for all of you with the affection of Christ Jesus.* [9] *And this is my prayer: that your love may abound more and more in knowledge and depth of insight,* [10] *so that you may be able to discern what is best and may be pure and blameless for the day of Christ,* [11] *filled with the fruit of righteousness that comes through Jesus Christ—to the glory and praise of God.*

[12] *Now I want you to know, brothers and sisters, that what has happened to me has actually served to advance the gospel.* [13] *As a result, it has become clear throughout the whole palace guard and to everyone else that I am in chains for Christ.* [14] *And because of my chains, most of the brothers and sisters have become confident in the Lord and dare all the more to proclaim the gospel without fear."* (Philippians 1:1-14, NIV)

"For this reason I, Paul, the prisoner of Christ Jesus for the sake of you Gentiles— [2] *Surely you have heard about the administration of God's grace that was given to me for you,* [3] *that is, the mystery made known to me by revelation, as I have already written briefly.* [4] *In reading this, then, you will be able to understand my insight into the mystery of Christ,* [5] *which was not made known to people in other generations as it has now been revealed by the Spirit to God's holy apostles and prophets."* (Ephesians 3:1-5, NIV)

Paul's life is his greatest epistle, just like your life is your most powerful testimony to those watching you.

> *"Are we beginning to commend ourselves again? Or do we need, like some people, letters of recommendation to you or from you? [2] You yourselves are our letter, written on our hearts, known and read by everyone. [3] You show that you are a letter from Christ, the result of our ministry, written not with ink but with the Spirit of the living God, not on tablets of stone but on tablets of human hearts."* (2 Corinthians 3:1-3, NIV)

Paul was originally arrested by the Jews and charged with taking a man named Trophimus, a Gentile companion of Paul's, into a forbidden area of the Temple in Jerusalem. (Acts 21)

Paul did not do this, but the Jews believed he did. They tried to kill him, but he came under the protection of the Roman soldiers. The Jews wanted Paul dead. The Romans were obliged to protect him since he was a Roman citizen and there was no proof of his guilt. Eventually, Paul was sent to Caesarea where he spent two years in prison. While there, Paul was examined by the Jewish Sanhedrin, Roman Governors Felix and Festus, and before King Agrippa.

If Paul had not appealed to Emperor Caesar, Agrippa would have released him. However, since Paul had appealed his case to Caesar he was sent by ship to Rome. The voyage took nearly a year to complete. When Paul arrived in Rome, he remained under house arrest for the next two years.

Paul lived in a rented house. In that house, he was free to move about during the day, but at night he was chained to Roman soldiers to prevent him from escaping. Paul's life was not one of luxury. He was a prisoner and his circumstances reflected that fact.

This is just a reminder that life does not always go according to our plans. I am sure that Paul never thought he would end up in prison. I would imagine that he saw himself going to Rome to stand in the

Forum preaching to huge crowds. I am sure he thought that he would preach to Caesar and the Senate of Rome and see great numbers of Romans converted. But, here he was in prison because he dared preach Jesus crucified and resurrected. No, Paul's ministry did not play out the way he surely thought it would.

A number of years ago when I was pastoring in the small town of Two Rivers, WI, I was approached by another pastor from a neighboring town and asked to consider taking his position once he retired. We would work together for a time and when he retired, my name would be presented to the congregation for a vote. My wife and I prayed fervently for wisdom and direction. After great consideration we surrendered our church and moved to a place called Sheboygan Falls.

Our timing was not the greatest for my wife was about to give birth to our daughter, Amy, during this time. We had been there a very short time; our house was still cluttered with boxes when this pastor and his wife asked to come over and meet with us. We were not prepared for what happened that night. They had changed their mind about our agreement and we were told we were no longer welcome in their congregation.

As they drove away and their taillights faded from view, I remember looking up toward heaven and saying, "God I trusted You, how could this happen?" I was a Minister without a church, bound in false accusations and rejection. Good intentions were rewarded with betrayal by people who wanted my ministry to die and for my family and I to disappear. It was professional and personal; it involved what I felt as rejection by my peers who did not know the real truth about the things that transpired. I felt that God had deserted us and hung us out to dry. I was all alone in a deep pit with no ladder to climb out. My reputation was soiled as false accusations spread like a brush fire.

I was desperate to survive and after a considerable struggle with bitterness I was determined to do what God called me to do and look for what God's purpose in this situation was.

God's plan was much broader than I had initially planned. It meant losing what I had and regaining a higher calling with a deeper vision and understanding of who I was in relation to whom I served.

Sometimes God takes away the familiar and changes your direction so you can reach people you would not have reached previously.

This life-changing event led me to an area that I would not have previously visited. We soon gathered with a group of people in a neighboring city who were also seeking direction and we were elected as their pastor. God blessed the work and we saw continued growth.

But, that's life, isn't it? The path of life never takes us where we think it will. Most things in life never go as we plan them, do they? Whether it's a relationship, a job, a vacation or a hobby, there are always changes to the plans we have scripted in our minds. What if everything in your life turned out the way you planned it? Would you agree with me that if we were left to drive the course of our lives, we would end up in bigger trouble than if we surrendered to God's will and let Him divinely guide us? You see, a major problem in navigating life is our limited vision. The course of our lives is constantly changing and unseen events are continually popping up around us. That's where faith comes in. Can I trust God to direct the events of my life even when I disagree?

The fact is, we rarely know what is best for our lives. Why? We lack all the information. We cannot see very far down the road. We do not even know what is going to take place in the next few minutes. We base our plans on limited or imperfect information.

As we saw, God had Paul right where He wanted him. God put him in prison so that he might expand his ministry. That sounds strange to our ears, and it is strange, but it accomplished God's purpose in Paul's ministry.

If you are saved, and you belong to the Lord, you are under His direction. He determines where the path of life leads you.

> Solomon said this, "*Trust in the LORD with all thine heart; and lean not unto thine own understanding. In all thy ways acknowledge him, and he shall direct thy paths*," (Proverbs 3:5-6, KJV)
>
> And this, "*A man's heart deviseth his way: but the LORD directeth his steps*," (Proverbs 16:9, KJV)

> Jeremiah said it this way, "*O LORD, I know that the way of man is not in himself: it is not in man that walketh to direct his steps,*" (Jeremiah 10:23, KJV)

Regardless of where you find yourselves in life, you must come to the place where you are confident of His sovereign leadership and direction. Otherwise, you will never have peace and joy as you walk in this world.

FOR THIS CAUSE I LIVE AND BREATHE

Paul says, "*For this cause I Paul ... for you Gentiles.*" Paul wants his readers to know that he is where he is for their sakes.

God had taken this strong, prejudiced, powerful Jewish man and saved him by His grace and sent him out to take the Gospel to the Gentiles. The Jews hated Paul for his preaching the gospel. They saw him as a traitor to God, to the Law and to his birthright. They wanted him dead! Thus, they did everything in their power to rid themselves of him and his preaching.

When Paul was arrested and carted off, first to Caesarea and then to Rome, the Jews probably assumed they were finished with Paul forever. They probably believed they had silenced this troublesome preacher. They might have stopped Paul from traveling around the world preaching, but their hatred against Paul had a surprising effect. Because he was locked up in prison, Paul had a lot of time on his hands. He used that time to write many of his epistles. He also used that time to tell people about Jesus Christ, and some, even some in Caesar's household, were saved. Philippians 4:22 says, "*All the saints salute you, chiefly they that are of Caesar's household.*"

Growing in the garden that God has planted you, even if it is full of thistles and weeds, God can cause you to flourish. Actually the light shines brightest in the darkest of spaces. So, while we do not possess a large quantity of Paul's preaching, we do possess an astounding wealth of theology from the pen of this amazing man. The Jews unwittingly helped place Paul in a position where the Lord could speak through him to the churches and we are still benefiting from their error today!

God used Paul to lay an incredibly important foundation for the church. God actually used Paul's imprisonment to expand his ministry. If Paul had been free to do as he pleased, he would have traveled around and preached from place to place, but because God was directing the course of his life, Paul ended up right where God wanted him. He ended up in the place he could do the most good.

This is just a reminder that nothing will derail God's plan! He accomplishes His purposes in spite of the sins and opposition of His enemies.

I'm not going to stop Him! You're not going to stop Him! Those who oppose the church are not going to stop Him. Our enemies will never even slow Him down. He is the Lord and He is in charge of all things at all times, no matter how it may appear to us, no matter the diagnosis, no matter the amount of public opinion!

GOD HAS YOU RIGHT WHERE HE WANTS YOU

God has you right where you are for it is there that you will bring Him the most glory. It is there that you will be prepared for the assignments He has for you down the road. It is there you will be made into the image of Jesus. It is there you will grow, be developed and shaped for His glory. He has you right where He wants you! The best thing you can ever do is learn to "grow where you are planted" and become all God saved you to be!

The Jews had arrested Paul, but he did not see himself as their prisoner. They charged him with blasphemy and wanted him killed. He had been detained for his own protection and sent to Rome at his own request, but he did not see himself as the Roman's prisoner either. He was waiting to appear before Caesar to face examination by the most powerful man in the world, but he did not consider himself to be Caesar's prisoner either!

Paul says that he is "*the prisoner of Jesus Christ.*" Paul saw himself as a man who lived under the sovereign control of God. He saw all the events of his life, the good and the bad, as being part of God's divine plan. He knew that the Romans could not hold him, the Jews could not stone him and Caesar could not execute him unless it was part of God's plan for his life. Paul saw himself as "*the prisoner of Jesus Christ.*" That phrase suggests the idea that Paul saw Jesus Christ as the ultimate cause behind his imprisonment. He knew that unless God had ordained it, he would not be where he was.

The Romans may have kept him chained, but Paul was bound to Christ by the very fact that Jesus had redeemed him from the deadness of his sins and given him a new life.

Paul was "*the prisoner of Jesus Christ*", bound to Him forever, regardless of where the Lord might lead him, or the things he might cause to happen in his life. Paul's perspective regarding his trials served to help his faith grow. If Paul had come to the place where he thought the Jews, the Romans or even Caesar was in control, he would have given up and fallen into discouragement and despair. Because Paul knew that everything he faced was part of God's plan, he could rejoice even in his trials.

> "*Now I want you to know, brothers and sisters, that what has happened to me has actually served to advance the gospel. [13] As a result, it has become clear throughout the whole palace guard and to everyone else that I am in chains for Christ. [14] And because of my chains, most of the brothers and sisters have become confident in the Lord and dare all the more to proclaim the gospel without fear.*" (Philippians 1:12-14, KJV)

PERSPECTIVE IS EVERYTHING

Perspective is everything! How you view the events of your life is more important than the events themselves.

> We are taught in the Bible "*to walk by faith and not by sight*", (2 Corinthians 5:7)
>
> We are taught that God is "*working all things together for good to them that love God.*" (Romans 8:28).

We are taught that we should rejoice in our trials because they help us to grow in the Lord.

> *"Beloved, think it not strange concerning the fiery trial which is to try you, as though some strange thing happened unto you:* 13 *But rejoice, inasmuch as ye are partakers of Christ's sufferings; that, when*

> *his glory shall be revealed, ye may be glad also with exceeding joy.*
>
> [14] *If ye be reproached for the name of Christ, happy are ye; for the spirit of glory and of God resteth upon you: on their part he is evil spoken of, but on your part he is glorified.* [15] *But let none of you suffer as a murderer, or as a thief, or as an evildoer, or as a busybody in other men's matters.*
>
> [16] *Yet if any man suffer as a Christian, let him not be ashamed; but let him glorify God on this behalf."* (1 Peter 4:12-16, KJV)

Paul understood God was working to accomplish the things that brought God the most glory.

Who is your warden today? Are you a prisoner of your circumstances or are you a prisoner of the Lord? Paul saw himself as being under the direct sovereignty of God Himself. He understood the truth that the Lord was the Master of all the paths of life.

> "*The steps of a good man are ordered by the Lord: and he delighteth in his way.*" (Psalm 37:23, KJV)

Job echoes this self-same sentiment:

> "*But he knoweth the way that I take: when he hath tried me, I shall come forth as gold.*" (Job 23:10, KJV)

If you are a prisoner of the circumstances of your life, you are going to be a miserable person. If you allow the actions of other people to cause you to refocus your faith, you will never have joy. If you allow the setbacks, the problems, the trials, the tribulations and the many other disruptions that can occur to cause you to forget who you are and what God has in store for you, your life will lose meaning. Remember you are being led every step of every day by the "unseen hand" of Almighty

God. If you do forget, you are going to have a difficult time surviving the potholes on the road of life.

However, if you can comprehend the truth, that all of life, including every good and every bad event, every mountain and every valley, every success and every failure, every blessing and every burden, and every moment of peace and every moment of pain, are all the work of God in your life, you can experience "*joy unspeakable and full of glory.*"

Our lives are not the product of chance, luck, karma, or accident; they are the product of the love of a sovereign God who controls all of life for His glory and our good.

> "*In whom also we have obtained an inheritance, being predestinated according to the purpose of him who worketh all things after the counsel of his own will:*". (Ephesians 1:11, KJV)

> "*Whatsoever the Lord pleased, that did he in heaven, and in earth, in the seas, and all deep places.*" (Psalm 135:6, KJV)

> " *Remember the former things of old: for I am God, and there is none else; I am God, and there is none like me,* [10] *Declaring the end from the beginning, and from ancient times the things that are not yet done, saying, My counsel shall stand, and I will do all my pleasure:* [11] *Calling a ravenous bird from the east, the man that executeth my counsel from a far country: yea, I have spoken it, I will also bring it to pass; I have purposed it, I will also do it.*" (Isaiah 46:9-11, KJV)

Our duty, even when we cannot comprehend the burdens and the problems of this life, is for us to bow before the Lord in humble acceptance of the path He has chosen for us. Anything less is a recipe for disaster. But, to do so brings both peace and ultimate blessing in the Lord's time.

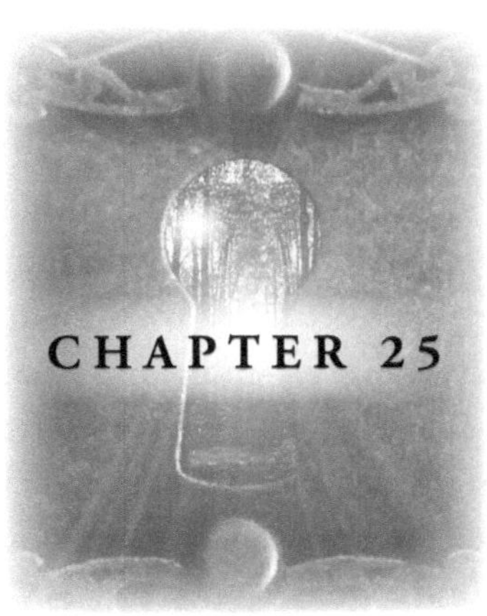

DIETER'S ROAD TO VICTORY

A number of years ago as a young minister I met a man that deeply impacted my life. I was attending a ministerial conference in Chicago and as we talked together, we began a lifelong friendship. We found we had so much in common through sharing our life experiences; it was like we had known each other all of our lives. Much like myself, he was experiencing his own medical challenges. We became like David and Johnathan in scripture. Through the many years we have known each other, we have kept in close contact. He now pastors a beautiful and loving church near Johnstown, Colorado. I asked Dieter to share an experience or two that would encourage you, the reader.

When I was a young man, I was living life for myself. Impulsive, reckless, and self-centered, I was moving full-speed ahead toward my own goals and dreams. When I was 21, however, that all came to a screeching halt! I felt a lump in my left cheek, and the doctors told me I had developed an aggressive cancer and did not have long to live.

As a young builder/framer in the seventies and eighties, I had been exposed to a lot of formaldehyde while cutting wood. Nowadays they use paraffins and non-toxic materials to make pine more resistant to rot, bugs, etc. Anyway, the news devastated me! I was angry, bitter, and I was overcome by fear, so much so that I broke out in neuro dermatitis, creepy crawling hives all over my body. It looked like an alien life form had taken over my body - all perpetrated by fear!

Folks, I was only 21 years old! I had my own construction business – I had dreams and plans! I had an incredibly beautiful girlfriend, Kimberly Ann, whom I wanted to marry! Here I had so much of life ahead of me, and suddenly God was taking that from me? I thought I was basically a good person … why was this happening to me instead of someone who was really evil like some rapist or murderer? Why not Charles Manson? YEAH, what's up with that God? Why did I have to feel like I was God's target? When I was told I was dying I opened the Bible and the Lord caused this Scripture to grow in font size times 6; it went from a 12 to 40!

> ***"Fear thou not; for I am with thee: be not dismayed; for I am thy God: I will strengthen thee; yea, I will help thee; yea, I will uphold thee with the right hand of my righteousness." (Isaiah 41:10 KJV)***

My precious parents, Gus and Brigitte Skowron, did everything in their power to help me defeat the cancer. They took me to different doctors and hospitals where they tried different treatments but nothing worked! Eventually, my journey led me to the Mayo Clinic in Rochester, Minnesota.

One day when I was walking through a park close to the hospital, my will finally broke. I realized that God was trying to get my attention. I fell to the ground under a tree and repented before God, weeping for all of the things I had done, for the attitudes I held that had caused people harm, and for the sins I had committed. When I got back to my hospital room, I picked up the phone and I called all the people I thought I may have wronged and apologized to them.

This Scripture came to me, **"Create in me a clean heart, O God; and renew a right spirit within me." (Psalm 51:10 KJV)** *No longer was I angry and bitter. I finally realized who I was. God was righteous. If I died from cancer, it would be just and what I deserved, or so I thought.*

The night before I was to undergo a major surgery on my jaw, my father, Gus Skowron, stayed in the room with me all night, but he did not sleep. As I drifted in and out of sleep, Dad prayed and prayed. I would wake up to find my dad reaching at my jaw and pulling away suddenly as if to yank the cancer cells out of my jaw saying, "In Jesus' name, in Jesus' name" over and over and reaching out, grasping the air, then pulling his arm back, as if he were removing the cancer. I would fall back asleep and when I awoke again, I would find my dad in the same position, doing the same thing.

The next morning, the doctors put me under expecting to do the surgery they had planned on, the total removal of the muscle on the left side of my face using a plastic inlay. Before they did the surgery they performed one final visual examination, but it was not what they were expecting. "I can't believe this!", a doctor said, "The tumor is shrinking; it's dying around the base." Overnight everything changed! Doc said to me, "I've heard of this phenomenon before but I have never seen it! It's a miracle!"

The Lord had healed me! I went from having no future to being able to imagine many tomorrows to come! I still love thinking about what my doctor said to me.... "I've heard of this phenomenon before but I have never seen it!" Other doctors were skeptical. They thought they should go through with radiation therapy, just in case, to make sure all the cancer died. They went through with the radiation and, through some kind of error, the radiation destroyed part of the tissue in my jaw. As a result, I can only open my mouth about 2 millimeters (.078 of an inch), which often causes people to stare when I'm eating in restaurants. Miraculously though, the Lord spared me from any speech impediment as doctors say I should sound like Popeye when I preach. When I sing they actually have to turn down the mic volume because I'm so loud! So even though I cannot completely open my mouth, you would never know it when you hear me speak or sing. Doctors told me I am the only case they've ever encountered like this; I should be malnourished and speech impaired. Guess what? I could lose 15-20 pounds!

I came through this experience a very different person - changed and hungry for God. I began praying daily and reading my Bible voraciously. ***"As the hart panteth after the water brooks, so my soul doth pant after thee, O God." (Psalm 42:1-2 KJV)*** *became my heart's cry, as I expressed, using the Psalmist's words, in a tune I wrote on my guitar.*

The Lord began to speak to me and lead me. Along with my wife, Kim, I began to walk through the doors the Lord was opening for me. Since then I've traveled around the country and the world, evangelizing as God opened doors for me to speak. Eventually, I felt led to start a mission work in Chicago and moved my whole growing family there. During those years, Kim and I had three children: Philip, Alisha, and Jeremy.

After four years in the "Windy City", the Lord spoke to us and told us to move back to our home state of Colorado. It was an amazing event! I awoke one morning with God's word in my mind echoing, "Send your father to Colorado and I'll show him where you are to go." Dad was amazing! He said, "Son, I'm out on the next flight!" Dad flew out, and through a series of God-orchestrated events, purchased some land to build a church in Johnstown. In a dream, I heard the name "Abundant Life Tabernacle." That was 25 years ago. Miracle after miracle occurred, as God began working and saving people in Northern Colorado.

Through the course of my life, I was healed twice more in my body – once of a completely unrelated form of cancer and once of ulcerative colitis - TOTALLY HEALED! There is no cure for ulcerative colitis. I have not been on sulfa drugs for over 20 years! The Lord has healed my body, saved my marriage, brought me through when people were coming against me with false accusations and evil reports, and through it all, I've come through as a man keenly aware of God's mercy. So if I boast, I will boast in the Lord!

As a result, Abundant Life has become a place where people can come for healing and to experience the mercy that only comes from God. All that are weary and heavy-laden are welcome. I've often said, "If it were my church, I could decide who is welcome and who is not, but it is not my church - it's God's church!" God has sent people from the north, south, east and west to the small community of Johnstown, Colorado!

If you ever want to quote anything that I say of myself say this, "I'm just proof God can use donkeys!" Folks, I've learned God's strength is made perfect in weakness. My objective is to show people the love and saving power of Jesus, the same way I was shown and to let everyone know that He is still doing what He said He came to do: ***"The thief cometh not, but for to steal, and to kill, and to destroy: I am come that they might have life, and that they might have it more abundantly."*** *(John 10:10 KJV) All glory and honor and praise to Jesus!*

YOU WILL CALL HIM JOHN

It all came as a surprise that day as Zechariah was ministering in the temple. The Archangel Gabriel appeared to this priest whose wife was barren and made an astounding promise.

> *"And there appeared unto him an angel of the Lord standing on the right side of the altar of incense. [12] And when Zacharias saw him, he was troubled, and fear fell upon him. [13] But the angel said unto him, Fear not, Zacharias: for thy prayer is heard; and thy wife Elisabeth shall bear thee a son, and thou shalt call his name John. [14] And thou shalt have joy and gladness; and many shall rejoice at his birth. [15] For he shall be great in the sight of the Lord, and shall drink neither wine nor strong drink; and he shall be filled with the Holy Ghost, even from his mother's womb."* (Luke 1:11-15, KJV)

John the Baptist, without a doubt, played a major role in spiritual history. He was to be the forerunner of the Messiah, "Jesus". That spiritual anointing was on him even before his birth. Jesus mentions, when talking of John, that no man born of a woman was greater than John the Baptist.

John's ministry was full of fire and success. People came from near and far to hear him speak and many repented of their sins and were baptized in the Jordan River. It seemed the climax of his ministry was the day that Jesus approached him at the Jordan and requested that John baptize Him to fulfill all righteousness. John saw heaven opened and the Spirit descending on Christ like a dove.

Jesus was the second cousin to John so no doubt they had many encounters as they grew up and developed a very strong relationship. This sounds like the perfect story; it has a relationship, success in ministry and God-given authority and blessings. However, there came a time when his ministry changed; John had no idea when he spoke to others that Jesus must increase and that he must decrease as to how great a decrease would take place. John had always been outspoken and unreserved when it came to doing what was right. There were none exempt from his scrutiny and Herod himself felt the barbs of John's words when John called him out for marrying his brother's wife after divorcing his own.

He was imprisoned and found himself living in a filthy cell. It was like taking an eagle who is used to soaring above the earth and putting it in a birdcage. John's life changed dramatically to say the least. Why didn't Jesus dispatch angels to open the doors of this cage? Why was heaven silent, did it not value this man who had given his entire life to the mission of heaven? It seems that when freedom and control are taken away from us, whether it be through declining health or any other reason, we begin to see the frailty of our human condition. John looked out the window of his cell and longed for what once was. He had been faithful in all of his duties yet now he suffered as a common criminal. Had he made a mistake? He thought, was I deceived, was any of it true? The battle of the mind is a battle ground where many fall. The enemies of discouragement and depression and suspicion are relentless in their attacks on a person's faith.

Like the constant beating of the surf on the shore during a storm, John's faith was affected. You must understand that his view from his cell was limited; he could not see beyond the scope of his limited vision. John sends several of his disciples to question Jesus regarding the doubts that plagued his mind.

> "*Now when John had heard in the prison the works of Christ, he sent two of his disciples, [3] And said unto him, Art thou he that should come, or do we look for another? [4] Jesus answered and said unto them, Go and shew John again those things which ye do hear and see: [5] The blind receive their sight, and the lame walk, the lepers are cleansed, and the deaf hear, the dead are raised up, and the poor have the gospel preached to them. [6] And blessed is he, whosoever shall not be offended in me.*" (Matthew 11:2-6, KJV)

The question John asked is hard to grasp. After all that has happened, after all that he had experienced and seen, how could he doubt? This great man of purpose and faith was human just like you and I. When placed in the prison cell of circumstances and suffering, his mind, just like ours, seeks logical understanding as to why and for what purpose. However, remember the view from your window is very limited. That is why Jesus told John's followers to go and tell him what they heard and saw in the ministry of Christ. John, you were never meant to be the main attraction. That is true for both you and I. It is all about the mission of the church. Each of us plays a different part but it is good to know that even though we may become confined that the work continues to go on. Jesus' last words ring loud and true, "*Blessed is the one who does not fall away on account of me*".

How easy it is to blame Christ for the cell we are living in. It is dark and confining, its walls restricting. There is very little sustenance in the cell of our trials. However, rest assured that God has not forgotten where you are and the manner in which you stand for Him.

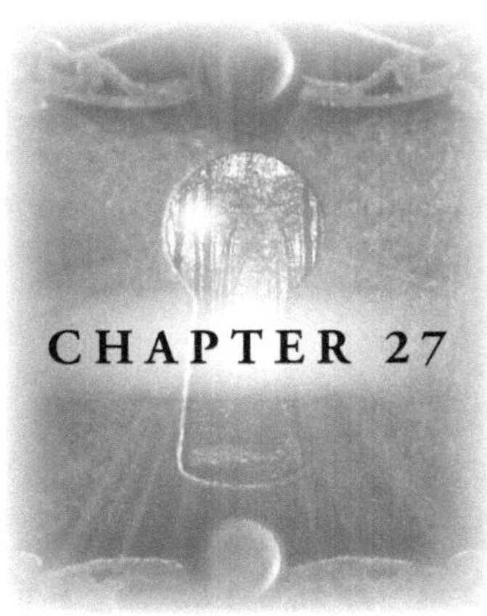

CHAPTER 27

THE DIVINE PROVIDENCE OF GOD

There are several basic ideas that men entertain concerning the working of God in this world. Some men profess the ideology of Deism. What, exactly is Deism? "Deism is the view that regards God as the intelligent Creator of an independent, law-abiding world but denies that He providentially guides it or intervenes in any way with its course of destiny." (Harvey, 1964, p. 66) Since Deists generally deny God's intervention in creation, it follows that they would refuse to recognize the biblical truths of incarnation, the atonement, the authority of the scriptures, miracles, the church, prayer, etc. Deism is false; however, because: (a) it makes no sense that God would create the world and then adopt a "hands-off" policy toward it, (b) it attacks the love, mercy, benevolence, etc. of the Creator, and (c) it expressly denies the scriptures and therefore leaves the great divine events of history unexplained.

There is also the mode of the miraculous. Many deny the miraculous saying that there is no longer any need for such intervention on God's part due to the fact that God's grace is sufficient to supply all our needs. I strongly affirm that the miraculous is alive and well and have received divine intervention in my own life, not only in the realm of healing but also supernaturally-given guidance. Some choose to embrace this concept solely as their view of God's intervention for mankind. Even though I subscribe to its important role in the world, I also feel that there is another way more often used in God's dealings with man; He uses the course of events that come into our lives to provide evidentiary changes in our character and spiritual well-being. This is encapsulated in the words "divine providence".

> PROVIDENCE DEFINED: The term "providence" is derived from the Latin "providentia," signifying "foresight". The word is used to denote the biblical idea of the wisdom and power "which God continually exercises in the preservation and government of the world, for the ends which he proposed to accomplish." (McClintock, 1968, 8:707)

"Providence concerns God's support, care and supervision of all creation, from the moment of the first creation to all the future into eternity." (Tenney, 1975, 4:920) The concept of providence, therefore, is opposed to Deism, which asserts God's non-interest in the world; additionally, it is the opposite of "fate" or "chance," which sees world events as uncontrollable and without any element of benevolent purpose.

When I look at God's creation I am overwhelmed at its divine order. From the celestial realm of the galaxies to the order of the earth, everything operating more precisely than a fine-tuned watch, the order of days and seasons, from the tides to even gravity itself. These patterns of order have allowed man to exist on earth without complete obliteration. Divine order is essential for our survival.

There are many instances in scripture of both providence and Deism. As we have already discussed Job, let us use his example of divine providence. Job, when we first met him, was an upright man who was consistent in prayer and faith. He was of outstanding character even to the extent that God pointed out his integrity to satan. However, God was not finished with Job's spiritual development and used this snapshot of his life to be incorporated into the Bible to provide edification and instruction for all those who would follow a similar trail in their own life. As the Bible states:

> "*These things happened to them as examples and were written down as warnings for us, on whom the culmination of the ages has come.*" (1 Corinthians 10:11, KJV)

In a sense, Job's life became, as Paul states, a living epistle.

> "*Ye are our epistle written in our hearts, known and read of all men:*" (2 Corinthians 3:2 KJV)

To understand the changes that have taken place in Job's life we have to compare Job when we first met him to the Job who stood at the end of the struggles of loss, pain and discouragement. If you have followed the biblical text, you can easily see that Job's relationship with God had grown to a depth that could not have been achieved without the struggle of suffering and loss. Yes, all his possessions were replaced and restored, save for his children who perished. He had more children but as a parent, there are some things that cannot be replaced. Job bears the grief of loss but also rejoices in the realm of blessing. Job, through the patterns of pain and suffering that are familiar to us all, had been able to have a relationship with God at a level that he hadn't previously. Nowhere in the Biblical text does it ever record a conversation between God and Job until the fiery trials consumed Job.

So, I can clearly state that God's will was accomplished through His intervention. Enemies took Job's flocks and killed his servants. The whirlwind destroyed his property and killed his children. His health was changed through the illness and boils erupted upon his body. There was even family strife via his wife's anger and rejection. His personal relationships changed because he was falsely accused and rejected by his friends. These changes to Job could only have come about because God allowed satan to have his way with Job - up to a certain point!

I laugh at times to myself when I hear people pray for patience for I know that God often uses events that occur in our lives to help us develop patience. So indirectly when things go worse in their daily lives, they question God as to why. I can almost hear God speaking back and saying, "Well you asked me to give you patience." Patience is something learned through experience.

CHAPTER 28

THE FRUITS OF SUFFERING

Now for you skeptics who may be thinking, "That was in the Old Testament! God operates completely different in the New Testament in the Dispensation of Grace." Well, let's look and see if that is true. When Jesus started His ministry at the age of 30, He chose 12 disciples and poured Himself into training them. For three years they not only sat at His feet but learned to operate in the same Spirit that Jesus did. They did this by healings and other miracles. However, it is interesting to note that when we look at their powerful ministries in the Book of Acts we see things not quite as exciting. We see the stoning of Stephen, the beating and imprisonment of not only Peter and the disciples, but Jesus' own beating and crucifixion. One of my favorite characters in the New Testament is Paul, originally called Saul, a person of Tarsus. When we first met him Paul was quite an unsavory character, one who persecuted and tormented the early church of God. When on the road to Damascus he met the risen Christ and had a life-changing experience which led to his becoming a very different man. However, when we read about his conversion and the reluctance of Ananias to approach him, God speaks clearly to Ananias and says these words:

> *"Then Ananias answered, Lord, I have heard by many of this man, how much evil he hath done to thy saints at Jerusalem: [14] And here he hath authority from the chief priests to bind all that call on thy name. [15] But the Lord said unto him, Go thy way: for he is a chosen vessel unto me, to bear my name before the Gentiles, and kings, and the children of Israel: [16] For I will shew him how great things he must suffer for my name's sake. [17] And Ananias went his way, and entered into the house; and putting his hands on him said, Brother Saul, the Lord, even Jesus, that appeared unto thee in the way as thou camest, hath sent me, that thou mightest receive thy sight, and be filled with the Holy Ghost. [18] And immediately there fell from his eyes as it had been scales: and he received sight forthwith, and arose, and was baptized."* (Acts 9:13-18, KJV)

The Lord instructs Ananias to go to Saul, for God has chosen him for a special purpose, and then says I will show him how many things he will suffer for His namesake. So Saul, I have some good news for you and I have some bad news. God has chosen you, that's the good news, but the bad news is this new life will bring about struggle, pain and suffering mixed with great revival. That, my friend, is often the recipe for a productive Chrisitan life. Sometimes we laugh together; sometimes we cry together. Nobody mentioned the suffering when I enlisted in the Lord's army. However, I have learned that the more battles I fight, the closer I get to God and the more confident I become in my faith and the promises of God.

What was Paul's opinion at the end of his life concerning the events of suffering?

> *"Are they Hebrews? So am I. Are they Israelites? So am I. Are they the seed of Abraham? So am I. [23]*

Are they ministers of Christ?—I speak as a fool—I am more: in labors more abundant, in stripes above measure, in prisons more frequently, in deaths often. [24] *From the Jews five times I received forty stripes minus one.* [25] *Three times I was beaten with rods; once I was stoned; three times I was shipwrecked; a night and a day I have been in the deep;*

[26] *in journeys often, in perils of waters, in perils of robbers, in perils of my own countrymen, in perils of the Gentiles, in perils in the city, in perils in the wilderness, in perils in the sea, in perils among false brethren;* [27] *in weariness and toil, in sleeplessness often, in hunger and thirst, in fastings often, in cold and nakedness—* [28] *besides the other things, what comes upon me daily: my deep concern for all the churches.* [29] *Who is weak, and I am not weak? Who is made to stumble, and I do not burn with indignation?* [30] *If I must boast, I will boast in the things which concern my infirmity.*" (2 Corinthians 11:22-30, KJV)

In this portion of scripture, Paul is defending his ministry and authority to those who have challenged him in the church. He mentions that his resumé is built upon the experiences of tribulation and victory. Would any dare compare their experiences to those of Paul? Paul realizes that the large impact of his ministry is built upon not only his relationship with Christ but on those trials of suffering and pain which affected every area of his life. Those times of physical and spiritual depletion allowed God to work in ways that showed not only Paul but the world that God was his strength.

I see this clearly stated in an instance where he sought God for a miracle of healing that was impeding, or so he thought, his ministry. God revealed that the trial he was experiencing was allowing Him to work through Paul in a divine and powerful way not possible in the fields of blessings but only in the valleys of hardship and self-denial.

> *"And lest I should be exalted above measure through the abundance of the revelations, there was given to me a thorn in the flesh, the messenger of Satan to buffet me, lest I should be exalted above measure.* [8] *For this thing I besought the Lord thrice, that it might depart from me.* [9] *And he said unto me, My grace is sufficient for thee: for my strength is made perfect in weakness. Most gladly therefore will I rather glory in my infirmities, that the power of Christ may rest upon me.* [10] *Therefore I take pleasure in infirmities, in reproaches, in necessities, in persecutions, in distresses for Christ's sake: for when I am weak, then am I strong."* (2 Corinthians 12:7-10, KJV)

This is a statement that you could not understand unless you have experienced the rewards that God brings from suffering. I relate to this statement very strongly as many times in my life when I felt I did not have the strength to go on, that divine source of strength was so evident. It was like a divine pair of jumper cables that provided me the power to start and face the day when, in myself, I lacked the strength.

David loudly declares as he reviews those valleys he has traveled in his life that if not for God's strength and intervention, he would not have made it through.

> *"If it had not been the Lord who was on our side, now may Israel say;* [2] *If it had not been the Lord who was on our side, when men rose up against us:* [3] *Then they had swallowed us up quick, when their wrath was kindled against us:* [4] *Then the waters had overwhelmed us, the stream had gone over our soul:* [5] *Then the proud waters had gone over our soul."* (Psalm 124:1-5, KJV)

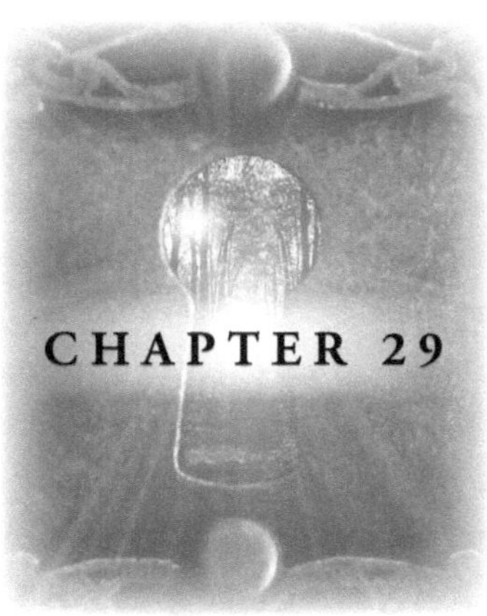

CHAPTER 29

JOHN THE BELOVED

There is one more character I would like to talk about at this point and that person's name is John. John of all the disciples seems to have the closest relationship with Jesus.

The disciple whom Jesus loved is specifically referred to six times in John's Gospel: he is always referred to as the beloved disciple or in other affectionate terminology.

> *"Now there was leaning on Jesus' bosom one of his disciples, whom Jesus loved."* (John 13:23, KJV)

This is portrayed in the portrait of Leonardo da Vinci's Last Supper denoting the affection shared between John and Jesus

However, as we explore the life of John we see the depth of revelation that John has in regard to Jesus' deity. The entire Book of John shows those glimpses of Christ's place in relationship to God Himself.

However, it is the end of John's life that I would like to briefly look at. He was born in 6 AD and lived to around 100 AD. He is credited with writing the Gospel of John as well as three epistles and the Book of Revelation. John is believed to be the only apostle that died of natural causes. It is also believed that he was boiled in oil but miraculously survived.

The second persecution of Christians under Domitian, AD 81, states, "Among the numerous martyrs that suffered during this persecution was Simeon, bishop of Jerusalem, who was crucified; and St. John, who was boiled in oil and afterward banished to Patmos. Flavia, the daughter of a Roman senator, was likewise banished to Pontus; and a law was made, 'That no Christian, once brought before the tribunal, should be exempted from punishment with renouncing his religion.'" *(Wikipedia)*

It was on the Isle of Patmos that John received, through revelation, the things that were to come upon the earth. Even though they had sought to kill him, God was not finished with John for he was to bring into the world a Book that was going to awaken the hearts and minds of people as to events that were yet to fall upon the face of the earth. No other person outside of Ezekiel and Isaiah had such a view of heaven as he did. But please be aware of the place he received these revelations. Patmos was the island of expulsion; it was a place of death and dying. It had no trees; it was a desolate place where Rome sent its prisoners. It was ten miles long and six miles wide. It is said that John received this revelation while living in a cave.

My mind also races back to Abraham and Sarah as they hold on to the promise the Lord gave them concerning their children and descendants. God had promised Abraham and Sarah a child.

Some of the greatest revelations that you will ever receive will be during the most barren and forsaken times of your life.

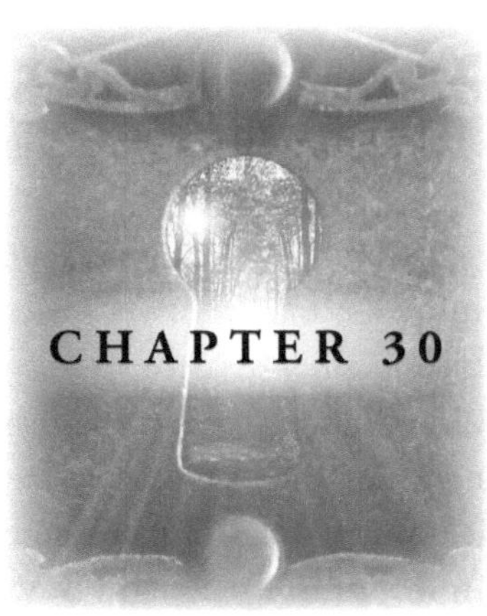

CHAPTER 30

WHEN IT LOOKS LIKE GOD FORGOT

Abraham was 75 years old when he received God's promise of a child. Due to his age, you would think the child would be immediately forthcoming. However, Abraham and Sarah had to wait 25 more years before Isaac was born! The Bible refers to Abraham as good as dead by the time the promise arrived, which means that the time of childbearing was no longer an option because of their age.

> *"And by faith even Sarah, who was past childbearing age, was enabled to bear children because she considered him faithful who had made the promise. [12] And so from this one man, <u>and he as good as dead,</u> came descendants as numerous as the stars in the sky and as countless as the sand on the seashore."* (Hebrews 11:11-12, NIV)

Sometimes your promises arrive over the course of time, according to the providence of God. But, rest assured, God does honor His promises. Ask David if living in a cave and running for his life is what he thought would happen after he was anointed to be king by Samuel. But in the course of time, he did take his rightful place on the throne according to God's promise. David had to wait nearly 15 years from the time he was first anointed by Samuel to the time he became king over Judah. Then it was another seven years before David was anointed king over all of Israel.

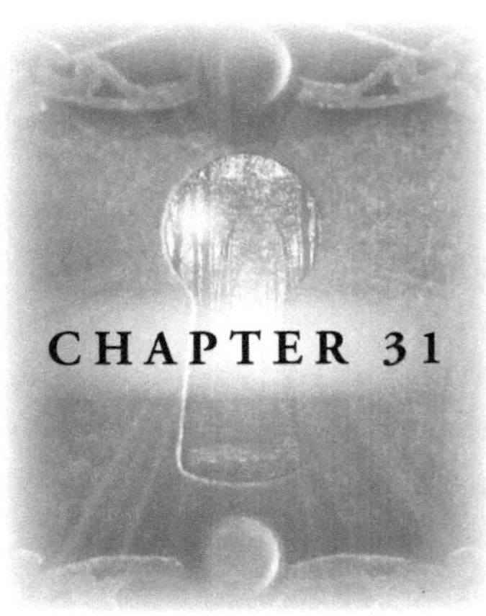

CHAPTER 31

HOW FAR ARE YOU WILLING TO GO FOR A MIRACLE?

I remember a story that, when I first read it from the scriptures, really caused me to step back and wonder if I was reading about the same Jesus who went about doing good and ministering to the multitudes, the same Jesus who healed the leper and touched the blinded eyes. He seemed to reach out to those whom society had cast aside and designated as hopeless. However, there is one story that stands out in contrast to many of the others.

The story is found in Matthew 15; let's look at it.

> *"Then Jesus went thence, and departed into the coasts of Tyre and Sidon.*[22] *And, behold, a woman of Canaan came out of the same coasts, and cried unto him, saying, Have mercy on me, O Lord, thou son of David; my daughter is grievously vexed with a devil.*[23] *But he answered her not a word. And his disciples came and besought him, saying, Send her away; for*

> *she crieth after us.*[24] *But he answered and said, I am not sent but unto the lost sheep of the house of Israel.*[25] *Then came she and worshipped him, saying, Lord, help me.*[26] *But he answered and said, It is not meet to take the children's bread, and to cast it to dogs.*[27] *And she said, Truth, Lord: yet the dogs eat of the crumbs which fall from their masters' table.*[28] *Then Jesus answered and said unto her, O woman, great is thy faith: be it unto thee even as thou wilt. And her daughter was made whole from that very hour.*" (Matthew 15:21-28, KJV)

Right away Matthew points out that this woman is a Canaanite. These people were not favored by Israel, to say it mildly. There were many such people as this woman who would not even try to gain an audience with Jesus for fear of the same response. However this woman's need was larger than her fear of the possibility of rejection. She was desperate and her desperation drove her into the presence of the disciples and Jesus.

The disciples demanded that she be driven away. She could have used this excuse to walk away and claim that Christians were hypocrites and really did not practice what they preached. She could have justified this by their treatment of her. However, desperation stomped on the hurt produced by her self-justification. She was desperate for the miraculous intervention on the part of Christ. She saw that Jesus had heard her cry for mercy, but there was no reply by Him - dead silence! He was, as it appeared, ignoring her petition.

When Jesus did answer her He declared that she is not the reason that He came to earth. He was sent to the lost sheep of Israel. This was her second opportunity to walk away and she could have and justified her actions completely. However, again, that would not have resolved her agony concerning the condition of her daughter. Sometimes Christians can seem so uncompassionate and wrapped up in their own circles of caring that they overlook those around them who are desperate for spiritual intervention. Oftentimes people do walk away from an impending miracle because of their past hurts and rejection. Is it possible that Jesus was testing the depth of her desire to reach that dimension of deliverance?

Jesus says something at this point that certainly would test her resolve:

> *"But he answered and said, It is not meet to take the children's bread, and to cast it to dogs."* (Matthew 15:26, KJV)

Did Jesus just refer to her as a dog? Why is He being so harsh and degrading? Will she storm away, will she wallow in rejection or will she continue forward with hope and faith that Christ will respond to her petitions?

> *"And she said, Truth, Lord: yet the dogs eat of the crumbs which fall from their masters' table."* (Matthew 15:27, KJV)

If that is how you feel about me Lord, that is fine, but let me remind You that even the little dogs get the crumbs from their master's table. I will be happy with just a small portion of Your mercy if need be, but I will not stop going forward until You grant me my petition!

Have you ever noticed on a cloudy and dreary day that all of a sudden there will be a break in the clouds and the sun's rays will break forth and shine so brightly? This is what happened next: the love and mercy that had been covered up by the clouds of testing broke through to shine directly on this lovely lady who would not stop until her daughter was delivered. Jesus was very conservative when it came to acknowledging certain actions. However, in this case, Jesus lifts His voice and used this Canaanite woman as an example to all Israel of overcoming faith.

> *"Then Jesus answered and said unto her, O woman, great is thy faith: be it unto thee even as thou wilt. And her daughter was made whole from that very hour."* (Matthew 15:28, KJV)

Thousands of years later we read of this woman's faith in scripture as a testimony of how God honors overcoming faith. Let me ask you a question if I may. Have you ever felt rejected by those who you expected would receive you and show you mercy? Has your past ever been brought up as to why God is not interested in helping you? Have you ever prayed and it seems that God does not answer you a word? How about feelings of worthiness; do you feel like the little dog living under the master's table?

This is not a time for you to withdraw into the corner of your life and blame the circumstances that have driven you there. This is the time to continue to reach out and receive God's blessing and to let your faith part the clouds of doubt so that the glory of God's delivering hand can reach down and reveal what has been there all along. His great love for you! So, if you feel like that little dog and feel no one cares, just keep on barking, for the master of the house has a place for you at the table of His mercy and grace.

CHAPTER 32

GOD WILL MEET YOU IN THE FURNACE

It was the year 605 B.C. and Israel, as was quite common, had turned their back on God; therefore He sent prophets to warn them over and over to turn from this path of wickedness. These prophets were sent to guide them away from the evil path they had chosen. God saw the end of sin and the judgment up ahead, but they willfully refused and punished the messengers sent for their benefit. A king called Nebuchadnezzar who ruled a nation called Babylon moved down from the North and completely destroyed the nation, leaving just a few to work the land. The remaining Jews were taken to Babylon and made to serve the Babylonians.

I would like to introduce you to four of these Hebrew captives. These four young men were called Daniel, Hananiah, Mishael and Azariah. They were believed to be teenagers at the time of their captivity. Nebuchadnezzar wished to assimilate the choicest young men taken from Israel into positions of leadership which he felt would speed along the acclamation of these captives. This was not only a blessing but a curse, for not only would they lose their Hebrew identities but their very names would be changed. Daniel's name was changed to Belteshazzar, Hananiah to Shadrach, Mishael to Meshach and Azariah to Abednego.

Things had radically changed in a very short period of time. Everything was gone, even their identity as men was changed as they were made eunuchs as Isaiah himself verified in his prophecy:

> "*Then Isaiah said to Hezekiah, "Hear the word of the Lord:* [17] *The time will surely come when everything in your palace, and all that your predecessors have stored up until this day, will be carried off to Babylon. Nothing will be left, says the Lord.* [18] *And some of your descendants, your own flesh and blood who will be born to you, will be taken away, and they will become eunuchs in the palace of the king of Babylon.*" (2 Kings 20:16-18, NIV)

They would never be able to have a family; they were to be totally dedicated to the purposes of the king. I do not need to tell you how they must have felt. However, the one person who gave them the most help was Daniel. He stands out as the leader, the encourager and the one strong in faith.

Sometimes in our lives everything changes overnight, not by our choosing necessarily but through circumstances we have no control over. We find ourselves overwhelmed with the change and we wrestle with, not only our identity, but our future and how it will be affected by these circumstances. For example, it could be a diagnosis that affects not only your location, but your identity and even your appearance and ability to exert the freedom that you once enjoyed. This is especially hard when you are young and you have not even had the opportunity to shape your goals in life before the playing field changes. Such was the case for these four young men.

As they faced these challenges, God blessed them and they increased in wisdom and knowledge. Suffering and trials will do that. They open up perspectives of ourselves that we have not seen previously as life was speeding by. It was then it happened, the trial of their life was on the horizon. This was going to be the mother of all trials for these young men. Nebuchadnezzar got it into his head that he was going to build a statue that was more beautiful and more glorious than any other. He was going to declare himself as a god and require all of those in his kingdom to worship it. There were to be no exceptions; if anyone failed to do so they would be cast alive into a fiery furnace and burned alive! Can you imagine their dilemma?

The one identity that satan cannot steal from you or any other man alive is your relationship with your heavenly Father. You can change your name and dress in different apparel; you can even be affected physically but you can never change the ownership of your life. You belong to God, and come what may, that cannot be allowed to change. However, the dilemma lies in this one question: Are you willing to go into the fiery furnace for your identity in Christ? That is what the devil will not give up trying to do; he wants to steal your spiritual identity. Nebuchadnezzar knew that these Hebrews were turning back to God in their struggle for survival as a nation and that could not be allowed.

Let me ask you a question. I certainly do not know what is going on in your life at this particular juncture or what changes you have been forced to accept - the loss of a loved one or the pain that is racking your body? This list could go on, but are you willing to bow down to the one thing that you still have and that is your identity in Christ? Now let me say, if you have not made that decision, you will find as I continue with this story, that it will be the best decision you could ever make.

The day came, the statue was set up, the people had gathered and the instruments were playing all the right songs to instill excitement in what was about to happen. There is something in this picture that is missing, however, as we read we ask the question, "Where is Daniel, or Belteshazzar?" He is the one that has kept this group of three together, but nowhere in the coming events could his name be found. These three Hebrew boys looked at each other and realized that this was the one challenge that they were going to have to face on their own. They could not find Daniel - where was he? Had he just bowed down like everyone else and they were unable to see him? This I do not believe for Daniel had shown his courage by standing up to the king previously. This was shown by his refusal to stop praying when the king commanded it, resulting in his sentence of being torn to pieces by lions.

> *"Then answered they and said before the king, That Daniel, which is of the children of the captivity of Judah, regardeth not thee, O king, nor the decree that thou hast signed, but maketh his petition three times a day. [14] "Then the king, when he heard these words, was sore displeased with himself, and set his heart on Daniel to deliver him: and he laboured till the going down of the sun to deliver him. [15] "Then these men assembled unto the king, and said unto the king, Know, O king, that the law of the Medes and Persians is, That no decree nor statute which the king establisheth may be changed.*
>
> *[16] "Then the king commanded, and they brought Daniel, and cast him into the den of lions. Now the king spake and said unto Daniel, Thy God whom thou servest continually, he will deliver thee." (Daniel 6:13-16, KJV)*

The day will come when each one of us must stand alone and make a decision that will affect the rest of our lives. In Daniel's case there was no real decision to be made. His dedication and consecration to God had been established long before this decree was made and it would not be changed. God's law trumps man's law. God is in charge and even though you find yourself facing similar situations you must hold onto your faith and relationship with God. Your greatest asset in struggle is your communication with God, which comes through prayer.

So you may be thinking, "What's going on with Shadrach, Meschach, and Abednego now that the music has stopped and the trumpets are sounding the call to worship?" Well my friend, everyone is doing what is expected; they're bowing before Nebuchadnezzar's statue. That is, all except for three young men. They stick out like sore thumbs;

you can't help but see them. They are standing out in defiance to the pressures of acceptance and approval from a kingdom void of God. I dare say you may only see three but all heaven was there that day to watch these three young men who had lost everything but their integrity and faith in God. The king is flabbergasted. "What do you mean you will not bow down after all I have done for you?" I am sure they are thinking the opposite. They were taken prisoners and made eunuchs never to marry or raise a family or carry on their name. Satan will ruin your life throwing you the scraps of a mediocre existence and when you resist him, he will try to make you feel like you're indebted to him. Satan will oftentimes give you one last chance to conform.

> *"Then Nebuchadnezzar in his rage and fury commanded to bring Shadrach, Meshach, and Abednego. Then they brought these men before the king.*
>
> *14 Nebuchadnezzar spake and said unto them, Is it true, O Shadrach, Meshach, and Abednego, do not ye serve my gods, nor worship the golden image which I have set up? 15 Now if ye be ready that at what time ye hear the sound of the cornet, flute, harp, sackbut, psaltery, and dulcimer, and all kinds of musick, ye fall down and worship the image which I have made; well: but if ye worship not, ye shall be cast the same hour into the midst of a burning fiery furnace; and who is that God that shall deliver you out of my hands?*
>
> *16 Shadrach, Meshach, and Abednego, answered and said to the king, O Nebuchadnezzar, we are not careful to answer thee in this matter. 17 If it be so, our God whom we serve is able to deliver us from the burning fiery furnace, and he will deliver us out of thine hand, O king. 18 But if not, be it known unto thee, O king, that we will not serve thy gods, nor worship the golden image which thou hast set up."* (Daniel 3:13-18, KJV)

There is no room in this comment for interpretation; it's pretty clear, we can change our clothes, our names, our location but we cannot change to whom we belong and whom we serve. God can deliver! Stop here! Did you catch that? A fiery furnace cannot thwart God's will for us. You see, God can do one of three things: He can deliver us right now from the enemy's hand, He can deliver us from the fire, or lastly, He can lift us away from the enemy's stronghold and place us in the kingdom of heaven.

Now there is a difference between the person who says they do not fear hell's fire and these three Hebrew boys who were getting ready to be thrown alive into a fire that is so strong and hot that you could feel it from a great distance away. The scripture declares that those soldiers who were commanded to throw these boys in the furnace were themselves, consumed by the fire. Those who say they are not afraid of hell's fire cannot smell the smoke or feel the heat or they would not so casually make that statement. These three could see their judgment from where they stood. As they walked they knew that if God did not intercede, they would surely be consumed by the fire and die. For this, they were prepared as much as any person could be.

Did they fear death? Of course, but they truly trusted the God of their fathers. You must realize, outside of themselves, they had no external support. There were no shouts or accolades of encouragement. Daniel was not there as I am assuming. But rest assured, it was not what they did not see that drove them on; no doubt God gave them extra strength and unction to make that long walk to what many assumed would be a terrible end.

Then the most amazing thing happened! As the soldiers approached the furnace the heat was so intense it consumed them, however, the Hebrew boys felt nothing. They stood amidst the flames and they were not consumed - it could be that it was cooler in the furnace than it was for those watching.

When they were walking around, it's then that they ran into the One that had stood by their side throughout this entire scenario. This is the unseen element that we often neglect to consider when we are figuring out the odds of our situation. God not only opened their eyes to His presence, but He allowed all present to see His divine appearance and miraculous deliverance. I dare say, in all the years that they had spent on earth they had never had such an intimate encounter with God as they had at that moment. I can only imagine the conversation that was taking place in the furnace. What was meant to kill them had only allowed them to see the Master of their life in a way they had never seen Him before.

That day the heart and mind of this great King Nebuchadnezzar was so moved that he uttered these words and changed the law so anyone who had the faith of these three young Hebrew men would never have to fear being persecuted in the future:

> *"Then Nebuchadnezzar the king was astonished, and rose up in haste, and spake, and said unto his counsellors, Did not we cast three men bound into the midst of the fire? They answered and said unto the king, True, O king.* [25] *He answered and said, Lo, I see four men loose, walking in the midst of the fire, and they have no hurt; and the form of the fourth is like the Son of God.* [26] *Then Nebuchadnezzar came near to the mouth of the burning fiery furnace, and spake, and said, Shadrach, Meshach, and Abednego, ye servants of the most high God, come forth, and come hither. Then Shadrach, Meshach, and Abednego, came forth of the midst of the fire.*
>
> [27] *And the princes, governors, and captains, and the king's counsellors, being gathered together, saw these men, upon whose bodies the fire had no power, nor was an hair of their head singed, neither were their coats changed, nor the smell of fire had passed on them."* (Daniel 3:24-27, KJV)

Look at the astonishment upon their faces, as they are lifted on the shoulders of those who were intent upon their death. That day every Hebrew went home with praise on their lips to the living God of Israel. I need to point out to you that your circumstance is not solely about your life, but the lives of those around you. How you live your life and how you face death affects those who are on the path behind you.

This is the message of this book. What you thought was meant for your harm is not only going to give you a perspective of God as you have never experienced, it is also going to affect those outside your trial who are directly impacted by your actions. God often reveals Himself to people during a time of their greatest need. That's why people who have been in the furnace will always be different after the epiphany of God's appearance in their tribulation. It is not always a visible appearance, but it will be a visitation that you will never forget.

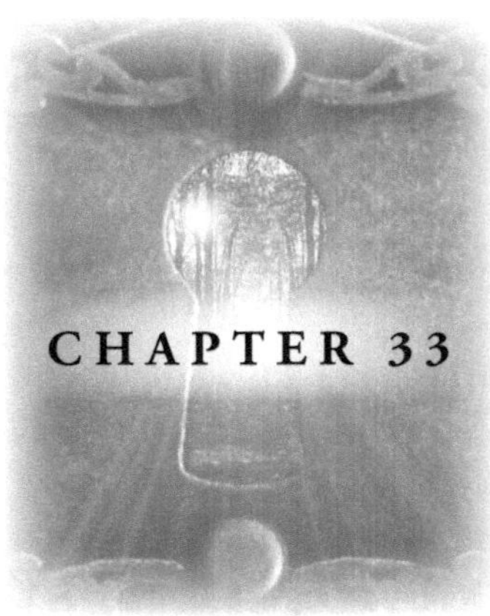

CHAPTER 33

WHEN GOD STEPS IN

I would like to take you back to the beginning, the beginning of all recorded history to where the world began and we met God for the very first time. What we call "earth" was a place of confusion; there was no order and nothing would make any sense to the onlooker. Let's look at the very first verses in the Bible:

> 1 *When God began creating the heavens and*
> *the earth,* 2 *the earth was a shapeless, chaotic mass,*
> *with the Spirit of God brooding over the dark vapors.*
> 3 *Then God said, "Let there be light." And light*
> *appeared.* (Genesis 1:1-3 TLB)

I want to make clear from the very beginning that God is a God of order and purpose. Everything He does or does not do has meaning and a purpose whether it be the creation of a world or the creation of a life. Everything is created with purpose. Your existence on this earth has a purpose. You will soon find out that I do not believe that the things we see and feel on this earth came about without direction and order.

Notice in verse 2 as we see God brooding over the chaos of what was yet to be unveiled by the direction of His voice. Now as much as I would like to, I am not going to go through the days of creation. I want to focus solely on these first three verses in our Bible. I see them as the blueprint for everything that is about to follow. God does not like disorder and confusion.

> [33] *For God is not the author of confusion but of peace,* (1 Corinthians 14:33 NKJV)

Our lives are very much like what we see here in Genesis. Before God steps in, our lives have no meaning, no purpose, no direction and most of all, no order. Life has no meaning without Him, and without Him our direction is at the very best muddied and confusing. When our society takes God out of the equation of life, life loses all meaning and direction. It's like looking through a snowstorm and trying to find your way to a place you are not even sure exists.

Before God brings order he always brings revelation of a particular condition. In Genesis he shows the confusion through the light of revelation. In our lives God first reveals our condition through the light of revelation before he brings the beginning of meaning and order. For instance an ant may feel great about his size until he stands next to an elephant. When man sees the revelation of God's purity and order he realizes the real condition of his or her life. Just realizing that fact does not in itself bring order; it solely shows the need a person has for godly intervention. Again I do not believe the order evolves from disorder without intervention on God's part. Currently in the news the world has been turned upside down and markets have crashed over a little virus that has brought world wide disorder. Up to this point man felt that he was in control of his destiny but now realizes that without intervention from the scientific community life as we know it is threatened.

It may be in your life that this scenario played out in a similar way. You felt in control of your life until some rebel cells attacked your body and life overnight changed completely. You realized how truly helpless you were in your own abilities and the limited abilities of others.

Confusion entered into the realm of your existence like a tsunami. The message I want to bring to you through this chapter is that God steps into confusion if He is invited and brings about meaning and order. With these two things in place the flood of fear is driven back and hope is shored up so your life has restored meaning.

The Bible, if I could boil it down to just a few phrases or words, could be stated this way: God created order, God created man from this order. Man turned from God and brought disorder and brought into paradise confusion and darkness. God sought out man and revealed his true condition. Man called out to God and He removed the disorder and once again rebuilt order into man's life, step by step leading him back toward godly fellowship and paradise.

I know this sounds very bare bones in the way it's written and maybe oversimplified, yet it has played out in truth throughout eternity. Man never sees the extent of his disorder until the light of revelation shows true weakness and confusion which comes through our human condition.

Even as Christians we will go through periods of disorder when nothing makes sense. For example, for three and one half years the disciples of Christ walked with Him. Everything during this time seemed to progress well in Christ's outreach to the suffering and disillusioned. They witnessed miracles that excited their faith and propelled them to truly believe that Jesus was the King prophesied to come who would sit upon the throne of David. You can see this in their questions:

> [6]*When they therefore were come together, they asked of him, saying, Lord, wilt thou at this time restore again the kingdom to Israel?* (Acts 1:6, KJV)

The above question was asked just before His ascension. They had witnessed His death and now His resurrection. Jesus had reviewed with them once again the prophecies concerning these things. They were well aware of the prophecy which spoke of Christ's return to the earth. Now they looked at each other, smiled and said, "This is what we have been waiting generations for." Jesus would be King and they would reign with Him. Instead they were told to abide in Jerusalem until they were endowed with power from on high. Then, right before their eyes, He ascended up into the clouds and was seen no more. In their minds He had come only to leave again. They were once again alone. We, like them, often in our lives see the promise but error in the order of receiving it. They waited 10 days in Jerusalem as Christ commanded and on the Day of Pentecost, the Spirit of God fell upon them and they were all filled with His Spirit. Jesus had told them He would never leave them or forsake them. It's then that they understood His being with them would now change to His being in them. Now what Jesus said in John 14 made sense:

> *At that day ye shall know that I am in my Father, and ye in me, and I in you.* (John 14:20 KJV)

God has established both an unchanging as well as an ever-changing order for His creation. Just as the world has turned at 1,000 miles an hour since the beginning of time and just as the seasons change each year, you need to learn that not everything follows the order in which you would like it to.

Living in Wisconsin I would like spring 12 months a year but I know that this will never happen for God has ordained the revolving and tilting of not only our little planet called Earth but those planets that revolve around our Sun.

Those disciples never did reign with Christ on earth. It is said that all but one were martyred for their faith and testimony. Does that mean that God was powerless to help them or that He cared not about their suffering. Not at all for that time is yet to come in the divine order of God's plan. God walked with them and carried them through their suffering for His spirit was in them and one day would resurrect them from their graves and carry them to the promises foretold in the Old Testament.

Take Joseph for instance, God gave him a dream in Genesis 37:

> *5 Joseph had a dream, and when he told it to his brothers, they hated him all the more. 6 He said*

to them, "Listen to this dream I had: 7 We were binding sheaves of grain out in the field when suddenly my sheaf rose and stood upright, while your sheaves gathered around mine and bowed down to it." 8 His brothers said to him, "Do you intend to reign over us? Will you actually rule us?" And they hated him all the more because of his dream and what he had said.

9 Then he had another dream, and he told it to his brothers. "Listen," he said, "I had another dream, and this time the sun and moon and eleven stars were bowing down to me." 10 When he told his father as well as his brothers, his father rebuked him and said, "What is this dream you had? Will your mother and I and your brothers actually come and bow down to the ground before you?" (Genesis 37:5-10 NIV)

Just as happened with the disciples of Christ, Joseph did not immediately receive the fulfillment of this God-given promise. Quite the opposite, his brothers sought to kill him but instead sold him into slavery, as a slave he was accused of sexual assault falsely and cast into prison. For roughly 15 years Joseph was not one step closer to receiving these promises than he was the day he received them. Now a casual reader may not see how God had devised a plan and set in place an order to bring him to the place where he would ascend into the second most powerful position in the known world. Each step involved Joseph's trust in God's promises. Joseph kept his eyes on the promises of God and not the circumstances that surrounded him. He lived a life of integrity even in the squalor of confinement and suffering. Through the order of God a butler and a baker were cast into prison alongside Joseph. They each were also given a dream to which God gave Joseph the interpretation. His interpretations were proven true.

It was when the great Pharaoh also had a dream that his wiseman could not interpret that Joseph's name was brought before the pharaoh. In desperation the pharaoh ordered Joseph to stand before him and tell him his dream and its interpretation. Now that's a tall order to fill.

He must tell the pharaoh what he dreamed and then its interpretation. Only God could do this and that is what he did, for he gave Joseph a revelation of the dream and its interpretation. Pharaoh was so overjoyed not only at the wisdom of Joseph but at the warning it provided to the nation of Egypt that he made Joseph second in command to himself.

From a slave to a prince in one day. God's plans are not always carried out in a way in which we would have them done. But they are always completed. Joseph's brethren and father did one day bow before him and he became a provider for the family of Jacob and Egypt became the incubator for a nation and people which were to be called Israel.

Was the suffering worth it? The glory is always greater than the pain when you put your life and fate in God's plans and not trust solely in your own.

Don't think for one moment that God has forgotten you in the prison of suffering. God has a plan, and God has a promise for you to trust in Him and follow him through the shadowy valleys of trial and He will take you to the mountains of God.

Do you remember the story of Elisha and his servant? They were surrounded by the Arameans heavily laden with weapons and chariots and Elisha encouraged his servant to see what he could not see. Let's read a clip from the text:

> *"And he answered, Fear not: for they that be with us are more than they that be with them.* [17] *"And Elisha prayed, and said, Lord, I pray thee, open his eyes, that he may see. And the Lord opened the eyes of the young man; and he saw: and, behold, the mountain was full of horses and chariots of fire round about Elisha."* (2 Kings 6:16-17, KJV)

How many times have I prayed, "Lord, let my eyes see those things which do not appear." Even if your support person does not show up, God has you covered. When the time is right, and only the Captain of the Lord's host gets to make that call, He will come and deliver you from the mouth of the lion who is intent on destroying you.

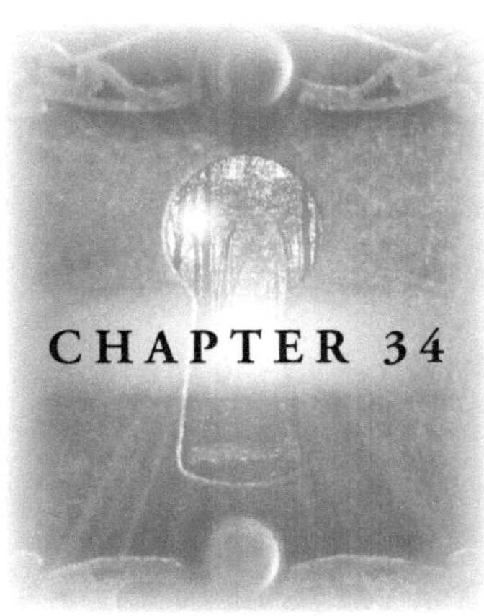

CHAPTER 34

WHY DOES GOD SEEM TO DISCRIMINATE?

One of the scriptures that many Christians lean on is found in Mark 16. Let's read it:

> *"He said to them, "Go into all the world and preach the gospel to all creation.* [16] *Whoever believes and is baptized will be saved, but whoever does not believe will be condemned.* [17] *And these signs will accompany those who believe: In my name they will drive out demons; they will speak in new tongues;* [18] *they will pick up snakes with their hands; and when they drink deadly poison, it will not hurt them at all; they will place their hands on sick people, and they will get well."* (Mark 16:15-18, NIV)

If you have not figured it out yet, you will soon discover that I am a pretty conservative guy when it comes to scripture. I believe that it's the handbook for humanity. I have and will continue to base my life on the words of this Book, the Bible. I have heard numerous messages about this scripture over the many years of my ministry. I have preached this message more times than I can remember. However, as I have worked in hospice for all these years, I have seen many patients holding onto this verse as they stepped into the realm of eternity.

"Why then, people ask, is it that some people are healed immediately and others, it may take weeks or months, while still others it seems not at all?" Is God a respecter of persons? Does He love some folks more than others? The above is a short list of questions that run through people's minds as they try to understand. Let me state clearly, I have been fortunate and blessed to have had an immediate healing of a brain cyst just before the knife was ready to cut. I can personally attest that God is able to heal! However, there have been many other times that I have prayed even more fervently and it seems, at the time, nothing happened.

I would like to give you a closer glimpse of the above scripture. Note how at the end of the verse it mentions that sick people will get well. Now that's a promise that you can take to the bank. You and I live in a unique time frame. We see the times and seasons; our clock seems to count down as we draw older and nearer to the time of our departure - 365 days a year, 24 hours a day, 60 minutes in an hour and 60 seconds in a minute. That's all we know; we know we are born, we live and then we die. It's unfortunate that in our culture we only see the speck of time that we occupy and not the total view of a glorious and endless time in eternity.

The average lifespan is 3 score and ten or about 70 years. I know as time passes, we are living a little longer. Now grab your calculator and enter 70 and see what percentage that is of eternity. Wait a second! We can't solve that problem because we do not have a number to compare 70 with. That's my point; eternity cannot be compared or computed by the human mind. That's the dimension that God lives in. When Jesus promises to heal us, it's a dimension and promise that spans not only our dimension of time but His as well.

"And God shall wipe away all tears from their eyes; and there shall be no more death, neither sorrow,

> *nor crying, neither shall there be any more pain: for the former things are passed away.*" (Revelation 21:4, KJV)

Notice that in the last part of the verse "the old order of things has passed away"; that's the dimension that we live in. In eternity, for the believer in Christ there is eternal healing in a place where there is no sickness, no doctors, no hospitals, no cancer, no death. If you're a believer, your healing is on the way. It may come in a moment, an hour, or week, or even on the other side of the door to eternity. When we pass through the portal of death, or if we are raptured up to heaven before death, we will look back at this time and realize it was just a speck in relation to eternity, a time that has no end. So hang in there; God has a Divine Plan and it will no doubt involve much more than you could ever think or imagine!

I heard a pastor share a story of an event that happened in his life. He had an elderly member of his church who was seriously ill and in the hospital. As he stopped by to see her he realized that life was slowly ebbing from her body. He prayed with her and as he was leaving the hospital over the intercom he heard this strange page, "Eleanor, your ride is on its way." That was the name of his patient. He was somewhat upset that they would say this on a public speaker system. Thus, in his frustration, he turned around and walked back to the patient's room to find her lifeless body. It was then that it hit him, that she had reached the time of her departure and that the Lord had made provision to come and release her from her diseased body and provide a transition to a dimension outside this earthly reality.

This reminds me of my own Dad's death. He had survived a serious surgery for lung cancer and the Lord had granted him seven more years of life. He was only 59 years old when he was released from suffering to meet the One he loved. The day he passed away was sadly the day I decided to step away for a little while. He seemed to be doing better and I yielded to the call of other duties, much to my regret. Of course, you know what happened; on the day of his departure, my mother was sitting by his bedside and his condition had changed radically in just a short time. His heart rate had shot up and his breathing was labored and then it happened. She looked at us boys as she described his death.

She said, "Boys, it was the strangest thing, he was lying in bed, unresponsive; he was struggling to breathe and then all of a sudden he sat straight up in bed. He was looking over the end of his hospital bed and he lifted up his arms like he was reaching out to someone and he was smiling and then he fell back and was gone." How I would have loved to have been there that day and looked into his eyes as he reached his hands up and smiled; maybe I could have seen in his eyes the reflection of the One I so desperately love. Friend, there is more to life than this short moment that you are walking through.

I have this little hobby that I have been doing for years. When asked if there is anything that I want from a family member's possessions after they have passed, I always ask the same question, "May I have their Bible?" Therefore, I was able to acquire my great-grandma Sisson's Bible. I had never had a chance to meet her because she had died before I was born. The only picture I have of her is one where she is holding her Bible. It is now a very prized possession in my collection of Bibles. I mention this story because while going through its pages I came across this poem which dates back to about 1864. It was handwritten and you may recognize another poem similar to it by an unknown author.

> "*I walked a road of sorrow, a road so dark with care and I was so, so certain that no one else was there. When I looked around about me on this road on which I trod, I saw two sets of footprints, my own and those of God*".

My dear friend, never think for one moment that you are all alone, even when there is no one with you as you are tossing in the darkness of fear and trepidation. There is a presence of the divine reaching out to touch your hand in that darkness bringing reassurance and hope for a new and brighter day.

"For his anger endureth but a moment; in his favour is life: weeping may endure for a night, but joy cometh in the morning." (Psalm 30:5, KJV)

FROM THE SEED'S PERSPECTIVE

It has always caused me great wonder to contemplate the transformation of a small acorn into a giant and massive oak, to think that something so strong and massive could come from something so small! This little acorn, whose weight could be measured in ounces, can be transformed at maturity into something weighing thousands of pounds and can provide shade and a habitat for birds and all types of different living creatures.

If you have not yet realized, you soon will, I have a vivid imagination. As I share my thoughts on this topic I pray that you might feel the heartbeat of the seed as it seeks to survive, for this story is our own in a sense. It contains a story of growth and the ability to overcome challenges as we reach our arms out toward the heavens, reaching for the light of the sun. It is a story of struggles and hardships mixed with victories. Eventually, the seed becomes a sapling and ultimately, a tree. However, have you ever considered this story from the seed's perspective?

This little seed comes into existence only because of another seed's struggle. It was a seed much like itself that had achieved its ultimate destiny that brought forth the opportunity for this little fellow.

The view from the treetops was breathtaking. The little acorn enjoyed the late summer breezes and the sound of the leaves as they brushed against him way up high in the tree. Gradually the days became shorter and the nights colder and he sensed a change was coming. Others like himself were falling from their lofty perches to disappear out of the sight of this canopy of changing leaves. The change brought feelings of anxiety as he realized others like himself were disappearing at an alarming rate.

He knew his own time was coming; he sensed it. Then the wind came and the branches swayed and shook; this little acorn tried to hold on to the twig that had supported him for so long but he finally lost his grip. He found himself falling and falling into an abyss of darkness and uncertainty. Then the sudden stop and surroundings were no longer familiar. He felt lost and alone. His view of the world was now limited as he laid there helpless on the earth as it sought to swallow him up.

This is exactly what happened over time; he found that he was descending into the black soil of death and decay. "How could such a lovely world so quickly turn to something so dreadful?", he thought. His beautiful shining body was starting to feel the effects of this damp and uninviting environment that he had suddenly been cast into. Oh, how he hated the wind that had shaken the tree and how upset he was with the tree that let him fall. It seemed there was no one to help and as he lay there in this condition, he felt that life would soon be over.

What the seed did not know was that a wonderful transformation was taking place! He did not realize that he was not just created to be a seed but a mighty Oak tree. However, for this to happen the life deep inside him that lies at the center of his existence needed to escape the shell of what was familiar. This transformation had to happen for this seed to shoot forth and reach toward the sky to embrace the sun and provide protection and growth for other seeds. It was what some may call the "cycle of life".

Deep down inside the earth, he could not see what was taking place inside him nor on the outside. Little did he realize that he would not know the difference until the day of his breakthrough when he would come forth from the blackness of change into the light of continued growth. The change that had taken place down deep in the soil would not stop when he once again came into the light of day.

To the seed, it seemed like eons of time that he was in the belly of the earth, but in reality, it was just a season. For the days were changing and the light shone brighter and stayed around longer. The memories of his time in the soil took a back seat to what he now was experiencing. He was completely different than he was before! He could not even recognize himself. He had many more appendages, each reaching on its own toward heaven. His little heart sang as he realized for the first time that the soil was not a curse but in reality, a conduit of change.

Once again he felt the stirring of the spring breezes and the warmth of the sun upon leaves that he himself possessed. His own roots reached deep down into the soil of corruption and brought stability in his growth towards the heavens. As he grew each day he found more and more life dwelling amidst his strong branches, for the little acorn was no longer an acorn but changing into the mighty Oak tree.

Have you seen yourself somewhere in this little narrative? Have you uttered the words of the acorn as he fought the fear and frustration of imposed change? I do believe I see a nod of acknowledgment. Now you can choose to stay an acorn, or for that matter like the caterpillar, you can be content to crawl upon the earth. However, you were not meant to stay a seed or a worm. You were meant to come through the metamorphosis of change as a new creature that would be able to leave the mediocrity of the past and achieve your place in the heavens. You were designed to provide safety and a haven for those like yourself who would follow the path of life.

So don't curse the soil of trials, for they can be the vehicle of change that transports you into a deeper dimension with God and a higher value of life.

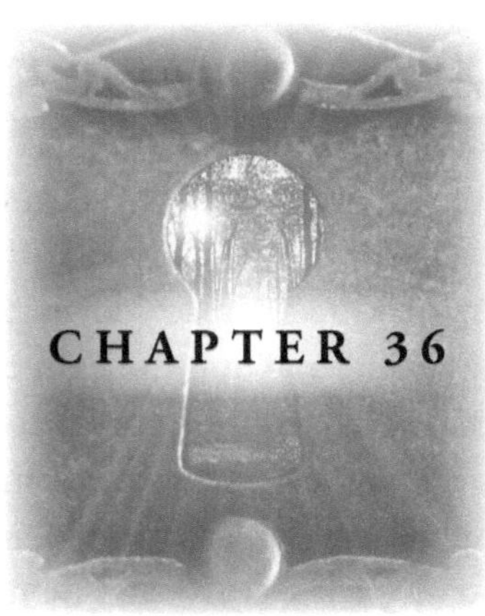

CHAPTER 36

OUT OF THE BELLY OF HELL CRIED I

> "*.........cried by reason of mine affliction unto the LORD, and he heard me; out of the belly of hell cried I, and thou heardest my voice.*" (Jonah 2:2, KJV)

There are certain things we do know about the story of Jonah. He was a prophet of God and that is most certain. The Book of Jonah was written somewhere between the 4th and 5th centuries during the reign of Jeroboam the Second. This would put the date around 786 B.C.

When God inspired the prophets to write he made sure that they recorded His words without bias or prejudice. God called a spade a spade. When we look at Jonah we see a man much like ourselves who had very strong opinions. To say that he was zealous for God would be an understatement. He loved righteousness and abhorred those who were wicked.

As we are reading this book, we certainly see his feelings concerning the Ninevites. In the ancient world, the record of the bloodiest and most vicious atrocities were attributed to the Ninevites. Jonah no doubt was a witness to some of these actions. He detested these people and what they stood for so when the Lord asked him to go to Nineveh and preach to them, he was more than reluctant. Instead of yielding to God's instruction, he chose to go in the opposite direction to avoid contact with the Ninevites. Therefore he purchased a ticket to sail on a ship headed away from where God instructed him to go,

Now I am not going to be too hard on Jonah, for like him there have been times in my life where I myself have not yielded to the direction that God had given me in His Word. Unfortunately, the road of disobedience is filled with obstacles that only frustrate us and cause us anguish. We withdraw inside ourselves to avoid hearing the voice calling us to turn around. Therefore, Jonah chose to go down into the ship and sleep even when the storm that was sent to wake him up raged outside its wall. Our rebellion always seems to affect those around us.

Those in the boat were frightened of the storm for it was unlike any storm they had seen before. They felt the pelting rain and the waves were nearly capsizing their little boat and Jonah slept through it all. The sailors in the boat woke him up from his slumber and to seek his God and ask for mercy. God always gives us opportunities to repent, turn around and head in the direction that He is sending us.

Jonah knew the reason for the storm, but he would rather die than yield to God's commission. How unfortunate an attitude to have when it comes to others. God has a way of using circumstances in our lives to cause us to see ourselves in a way that we normally wouldn't. Instead of changing his mind he told those on the boat to throw him over into this raging torrent of wind and water. He would rather die than obey.

God in His infinite mercy knew this event would happen and had specifically designed a great fish to swallow up this rebellious prophet. The fish did swallow him and in the belly of this fish, Jonah had time to reflect on the consequences of his disobedience.

The stench of the gastric juices in the fish's stomach was atrocious! Jonah was finding out it is easier to walk with God than it is to run from

Him. Jonah's words shout out his torment, "*Out of the belly of hell cried I, and thou heardest my voice.*" (Jonah 2:2 KJV) With a changed heart, there was also a changed direction. That is what repentance does; it changes the direction that we are traveling.

Some may say that it was unfair of God to bring such torment upon Jonah. Let's look at this differently. There were more than 120,000 people in the city of Nineveh. That would mean 120,000 lives were at stake for Jonah's prophecy mentioned that in 40 days God was going to destroy this city if they did not repent. These people's lives were dependent on him delivering this message. It was through Jonah's preaching of God's message that these people repented of their sins and received deliverance from this judgment.

Now, what does all this mean? How does this affect you and me? Sometimes the storms that enter into our lives change our direction. Let me give you an example. I was 20 years old, recently off of active duty in the service. I had been raised in a Christian home and followed those Christian traditions expected of me never really yielding, however, to follow God's call on my life. Through some bad decisions, I found myself in a dilemma - a place that I could not escape from. I was disillusioned with life and looked for a way of escape. I was going to throw myself over the side of the boat so to speak and let go of the most precious gift that I had ever received, the gift of life. I was at the door of death and reaching for its handle when I found a church door in my path to oblivion. It was alone in this little church that I wrestled with God and asked for help and mercy and forgiveness.

This situation was what brought me to my knees and caused me to change direction. That was 47 years ago! I prepared myself for ministry and after graduation, I pastored my first church in 1980. How many people have been affected by my ministry? How many lives did I introduce to Christ over these many years? Our decisions not only affect us but they also affect others that God intended to place in our path.

I have noticed that many converts to Christ have something in common. They have found themselves in the belly of hell and have cried out to God for deliverance. Trials and struggle can be a conduit for spiritual evaluation. If it had not been for that great fish, where would Jonah be? Where would those 120,000 people in Nineveh be?

I truly believe the account of Jonah is in God's Word for a purpose. It is not just another great fish story. It's there for you and I to contemplate and consider. Consider Paul's words:

> *"For whatsoever things were written aforetime were written for our learning, that we through patience and comfort of the Scriptures might have hope." (Romans 15:4, KJV)*

CHAPTER 37

HELP CAN COME FROM THE STRANGEST PLACES

It never ceases to amaze me how God intercedes in our circumstances, sometimes in the most unusual way. I am sure we all have stories that we could relate to.

I remember a time some years ago, I was attending college in St Paul, Minnesota and was heading home for Christmas break. I was a close friend of the cook who worked in our cafeteria; I actually interned at her son's church in Milwaukee during my summers.

She asked if I wouldn't mind, on my way back home from break, stopping at her son's and leaving her Christmas gifts with them. Unfortunately, she was not able to get all the gifts together until late in the same day that I was driving back. I am not so foolish as to offend a person who is as good a cook as she was, but it was almost 10:00 p.m. before I was able to get on the road. I was somewhat agitated as I am not a very good night driver and I knew I would not be home until the next morning. As I was driving, I heard a call for help over the Citizens Band radio I had in my car. A truck had broken down along the interstate and the driver was trying to get home before Christmas Eve. He mentioned that the truck would be towed and he was able to continue traveling on his own. I have a truck driving background and have always had a tender spot in my heart for those who do this type of work.

"Why not?" I said to myself. The company of this driver might help me stay awake and I decided to pick him up. I remember pulling up behind the semi and getting an uneasy feeling when two rough-looking characters walked back to my car. (I was only expecting one.) Well, I thought it was too late to change my mind at this point. We cleared out the gifts from the back seat and moved them to the trunk.

I remember praying and asking God for His divine presence in all that was taking place. It was more like a plea, "Please God, do not let them rob me or physically harm me." I was all wrong in my assessment of these two men. They looked like something out of a gang war movie, but they were both very polite. For the next three hours, we talked about our families and how much God played a role in our lives. I was able to share how much God truly loved them and how He desperately longed to be part of our everyday lives.

You could cut God's presence in the car with a knife. It was so powerful. I then knew that God had arranged this meeting and felt so glad that I had stopped to help. I remember how I felt the moment they exited the car at their destination, how this whole experience had unctioned my sense of God's presence and my joy in following His direction.

I remember after they exited the car, heading down the highway and saying out loud, "God I feel so close to You at this moment - show me your glory!" I do not know what I expected Him to do but anything would have been great. I was in the midst of that request and no sooner had I gotten the words out of my mouth when all the envelopes behind my visor with all the other clutter fell down and hit me in the face! I nearly jumped out of my seat and my heart was beating like a rock star's drum. I began to realize that maybe I wasn't quite as ready as I thought for God to display His glory.

Now, unfortunately for me these two men lived off the route I would normally have taken home, which was all interstate. I had exited the interstate and was driving through central Wisconsin. I was in the middle of nowhere. My initial plan was to stop and get gas about half-way home at one of the numerous truck stops along the way. It was then that I saw my gas gauge. It was empty. I had been so engrossed in our conversation that I had not paid attention to my gas supply. It was nearly two-thirty in the morning and I was nowhere near a city large enough to have a 24-hour station.

This happened at a time when we did not have 24-hour self serve pumps, the good old days when you didn't even need to get out of your car to get your tank filled. I remember praying out loud and saying, " Lord what am I going to do now?" I grabbed the microphone for my radio and quickly keyed it and asked for help in finding a gas station open at this time of the night.

Honestly, my friend, I did not expect any answer at all. Who is going to be up at this time of the night unless it was another trucker? I had not even passed a car for as long as I could remember. Then it happened, loud and clear and strong, as if the person were right next to me. This person had no idea of my location or the direction I was driving in or even the road I was on. The words went like this: "There is a gas station just ahead, and don't be worried, I am right behind you." I was somewhat stunned but thanked him. Sure enough, not more than a mile ahead there was a gas station open for business in the middle of nowhere, at 2:30 in the morning.

I pulled up next to the pump and just sat there watching the road to see who it was that had talked to me. No one came by; there were no headlights in the distance. It was then that I heard a voice that said, "You wanted Me to light up the sky, but what you really needed was gas." Well let me tell you, I began to laugh and praise God, for He knows what we need! Even when we're asking for something foolish, He comes through. I never found out why that station was open at that late hour.

You just don't know how God is going to supply your need, or who or what He will use to do it. Have you ever been desperate for divine intervention and wondered how you would ever get what you needed? Then all of a sudden God sends you exactly what you need!

I remember a particular service at a church in Milwaukee where I was interning; it was a smaller church and the atmosphere was quite casual. We were just starting our service when a lady stood up and said, "Pastor, I have to apologize but I have something that I need to share before I burst. As you know I have a limited budget and when it came time to come to church I did not know how I was going to get here. You see Pastor, I had run out of money before I ran out of month. My gas gauge was on empty and I knew that I could not make it here with what was left." I said, "Lord, I need to be in church today and I am going to step out in faith and trust you will get me there." "Well, Pastor, I got my things and got in my car and as I was leaning out to pull the door shut, I happened to glance down on the ground and what do you think I saw but a twenty-dollar bill just lying there on the ground. Well, pastor, I was able to fill my tank up with that money and I will have enough left over to buy a little lunch."

Now, this may not mean a lot to some people but to those that were there that morning, it caused them to rejoice with this lady and increased their faith to go the extra mile. Since that day I have heard many such stories of God's miraculous provisions.

However, it is not only money that God can give us when we need it. He can give us the courage to face the enemy of fear when our faith is almost gone. Some of the greatest things that have ever happened in my life have come at my weakest and most vulnerable times. Just remember, you may be asking God for one thing when He is getting ready to give you what you really need. It may be water from a rock as it was for Moses and Israel in the desert. This rock followed Israel through their journeys in the wilderness so that they never ran out of water. How about the baskets of bread and fish that one small boy donated from his lunch that fed the five thousand? Just don't give up because it may come from a place you least expect it. He may not always give you what you want but he will always give you what you need.

CHAPTER 38

WHEN OUR EXPECTATIONS CRASH AND BURN

Did you ever have one of those days when everything that could go wrong does go wrong? These days are especially hard to take when you had expected to have things fall into place. I was thinking of the Christmas story. What a beautiful concept! The Incarnation was planned from the foundation of the world to have God robe Himself in flesh, become a man and live among His own creation. The Incarnation, or the birth of Christ, was not an afterthought or a decision made in the spur of the moment. God knew even before He created man that there would come a time that He Himself would have to come and deliver man from his own evil actions.

The prophets such as Isaiah and Micah loudly proclaimed His arrival long before it ever took place. Isaiah spoke of His majesty and identity:

> *"For to us a child is born, to us a son is given, and the government will be on his shoulders And he will be*

> *called Wonderful Counselor, Mighty God, Everlasting Father, Prince of Peace.*" (Isaiah 9:6, NIV)

Micah speaks of His birthplace:

> "*But you, Bethlehem Ephrathah, though you are small among the clans of Judah, out of you will come for me one who will be ruler over Israel, whose origins are from of old, from ancient times.*" (Micah 5:2, NIV)

Now I mention these two scriptures for a purpose. The Incarnation of God in flesh was the biggest event ever recorded in scripture. For a world cascading toward destruction with no hope was given hope through God's personal and devoted intervention. His coming was promised from the beginning of scripture. God spoke to Adam and Eve as they both stood heads down and ashamed in His presence. Even though their actions reaped terrible and long-lasting repercussions for the human race, God placed in the heart of man a hope for a better day. For roughly 4,000 years of darkness man was waiting for that message of hope to arrive.

When that day came, the world stood amazed watching this story unfold and become a reality. We look at the characters that were chosen, the political climate, and the place of Christ's birth and we stand in awe as the story unravels.

The first character we meet is a man named Zechariah, an elderly priest serving in the temple. He and his wife had been married for many years. Unfortunately even though they had tried to conceive a child as long as it was possible, they did so without success. They had prayed for a male child of their own but the womb of Elizabeth remained closed until one day, that wonderful day, that the angel Gabriel appeared.

> "*They had no children because Elizabeth was unable to conceive, and they were both very old.*" (Luke 1:7, NLT)

It was the day that the lot fell on Zechariah to work in the Temple, a distinct honor which was cherished by any priest, but even more so by those in the twilight of their life. Gabriel appeared to Zechariah while he was in the temple. Think of it, an angel appears and begins to speak with you and the message he shares at that moment will change your entire life!

> "*While Zechariah was in the sanctuary, an angel of the Lord appeared to him, standing to the right of the incense altar.* [12] *Zechariah was shaken and overwhelmed with fear when he saw him.* [13] *But the angel said, "Don't be afraid, Zechariah! God has heard your prayer. Your wife, Elizabeth, will give you a son, and you are to name him John.* [14] *You will have great joy and gladness, and many will rejoice at his birth,* [15] *for he will be great in the eyes of the Lord.*" (Luke 1:11-15, NLT)

I am certain Zechariah must have thought, "After all these years I have prayed for this, you mean to tell me you are going to answer it now when I am at this age and time of life?" I do not know about you, but now that I am a little older, I do not relish the thought of raising a baby. I am thrilled to be a grandpa, but I am really not into child-rearing at this stage of life. "Why did you not answer earlier when I was more prepared?" Zechariah might have thought.

This child, Gabriel declared, would play a major role in the announcement and preparation for the Son of God. Gabriel tried to send home the fact that this was more than an isolated incident; the birth of this child would be part of a larger and more divine purpose and plan. It was not about whether it was the best time of life for Zechariah and Elizabeth, it was about a greater and much larger cause that affected more than just two individuals; it affected all humanity.

> "*And he will turn many Israelites to the Lord their God.* [17] *He will be a man with the spirit and power of Elijah.* *He will prepare the people for the*

> *coming of the Lord. He will turn the hearts of the fathers to their children, and he will cause those who are rebellious to accept the wisdom of the godly.* [18] *Zechariah said to the angel, 'How can I be sure this will happen? I'm an old man now, and my wife is also well along in years.'*" (Luke 1:16-18, NLT)

Zechariah was so conditioned by disappointment that it was hard for him to accept this promise even though he was standing right next to the Altar of Incense in the Temple of God, speaking to archangel Gabriel. This is the same Gabriel that had spoken to Daniel and helped explain his visions. Being a devout priest, no doubt, he knew who this angel was and his previous role in history.

So to be sure that even though it was not a convenient time for Zechariah and Elizabeth, it was the right time for the world.

Six months later this same angel, Gabriel, appeared to Mary. This was a young lady who was espoused to a young man named Joseph. They had, at this time, not consummated their relationship in that they were espoused and not yet married to each other.

Notice the manner of discourse at the angel's appearing. The angel's excitement does not seem to match that of Mary, or for that matter, Zechariah. How do you wrap your head around the news of such an unexpected event suddenly appearing in your life out of nowhere?

> *"Gabriel appeared to her and said, "Greetings favored woman! The Lord is with you!" "Confused and disturbed, Mary tried to think what the angel could mean.* [30] *"Don't be afraid, Mary," the angel told her, "for you have found favor with God!* [31] *You will conceive and give birth to a son, and you will name him Jesus.* [32] *He will be very great and will be called the Son of the Most High. The Lord God will give him the throne of his ancestor David.* [33] *And he will reign over Israel forever; his Kingdom will never end!"* (Luke 1:28-33, NLT)

Please note that the angel mentions the same utterance to Mary as he did Zechariah, "*Don't be afraid.*" This young girl was not educated, she was not married, she was not from a wealthy family, and she lived in the outskirts of obscurity. This is not how she had planned her new life; it is certainly not a convenient time for her to be pregnant. To be pregnant without a husband was a very humiliating event. What was she going to do? She was going to give birth to the Son of the Most High.

Can you imagine your own shock, at not only this supernatural appearance, but the magnitude of the announcement? Her young and innocent mind is racing out of control. Fear is tightening her chest and she finds it hard to breathe. "Do not be afraid Mary, you are highly favored." God has chosen you to bear the child of the Almighty because He knows that you are able to bear it, not only in your womb, but the responsibilities that come with it.

She was excited; she felt honored and humbled at the same time, to think that God would choose her. However, with this honor came hardship and separation. She had to face Joseph, the love of her life. What if he did not believe her when she told him why she was pregnant, who the father was, and for that matter, who the Child was and what role He would play in history? He was the Savior of the world! He was God incarnate in a human form. That little Child was going to be subject to her child-rearing. For a girl of roughly thirteen years old, this is a lot to take in.

Little did she know the hardship she would endure, however, in her future. Not only the hardship, but the relationship she would develop with the Almighty God in Christ.

She would be there when He was delivered and she would be there as He was crucified. She would be there at His resurrection and then she would witness His ascension. No other person on earth could say that they had a more intimate relationship with Jesus than that of Mary. She thought of the responsibility that was now on her shoulders.

Do you think that God had not first evaluated His choices of the participants of this story of the ages? Would you drop off your only child with someone you did not trust or who you thought was not capable of watching your child?

In like manner, God has chosen you, my friend, to play a part in these last days. He is entrusting you with the Message of Salvation. The time may not be convenient and the requests may have been many and scattered throughout the many years of unanswered petitions. Yet, God is still reaching out to you and telling you to not be afraid or overwhelmed by the magnitude of what is taking place in and around you. You may not feel you have the pedigree of others, nor the means, but you do have something that is important in the plan of God for the world. You may feel like your life has run its course and you are getting ready to hang up the closed sign on the door to your life, however, you may be surprised at what is coming next.

I have seen many people put the promises on the back burner of their lives, waiting for a more convenient time that may never come. You may even have an attitude that says, "But it is so much easier for others and your life is too difficult for you to succeed." You may even feel that God is a respecter of persons. Well, how do you think it worked out for Mary and Joseph? Joseph had his own visitation telling him to take onto himself Mary, for that which was conceived in her womb was of the Holy Ghost. How did life work out for the royal family? The political climate was in turmoil. There was a decree by Caesar Augustus for all families to report to the city of their fathers for a census.

> "*At that time the Roman emperor, Augustus, decreed that a census should be taken throughout the Roman Empire.*" (Luke 2:1, NIV)

The timing of this decree could not have been worse, for Mary was near the time of her delivery. Can you imagine the trip from Nazareth to Bethlehem? The trip was 90 miles, traveling south along the flatlands of the Jordan River, then west over the hills surrounding Jerusalem, and onto Bethlehem. It was a grueling trip by anyone's standards!

Now let's look at this story more closely. We already know that God had planned this event from the beginning of time. Had He forgotten that this decree was going to be made at the time that Christ was going to be born? Had He not taken into consideration that the inn might be full that night with all of the travelers? For Mary and Joseph, those highly favored of God, may not have felt so favored as they traveled on this long journey.

Joseph no doubt was a great and caring husband. He saw Mary's discomfort; he heard her pleas for a place to give birth as he knocked on every door available to find lodging for his wife, who now was in the midst of labor pains. Really, the best you can do is a cave that you call a stable, no ventilation, dampness and all sorts of smells? This is the place that God prepared for His entrance into the world! None of this makes sense to our human reasoning. However, God has a plan that exceeds the scope of our limited view of place, time and situation, for that night the angels sang praises on the hillsides of Bethlehem. The wise men were following celestial signs in the heavens to the place of His birth. God's ways, God's plans are not always easily understood and their purposes may never be found out, but rest assured, God has a plan and it is a plan that does not always cater to our convenience or our time frame. So stop trying to understand His timing or His motives. His love will always lead you through to the place of delivery of revelation and understanding.

CHAPTER 39

WHY GOD, HAVE YOU DONE THIS TO ME?

I remember the day so well! It was a bright sunny morning and I was driving into the parking lot of Holy Family Hospital in Manitowoc, Wisconsin. I was excited with this new aspect of my ministry in Hospital Chaplaincy. I had just started pastoring my first church in a little city called Two Rivers on the shores of Lake Michigan in eastern Wisconsin and was now volunteering in the evenings as a chaplain. It seemed as if I had waited forever for this new aspect of my ministry. I had my degree on the wall and felt I was ready to face all the challenges of spiritual care as a pastor and chaplain.

I was overjoyed to finally be doing what I felt I was called to do. Little did I know that day, that an event would take place that would change my life. As I picked up the hospital's admission sheet and planned my activities for the evening, I saw that we had a young lady on the medical-surgical floor who was recently out of surgery. I decided that this would be my first stop.

As I remember this event, I realize how naive I was as I knocked on the door and asked to come in. I had not prepared myself for this visit; I knew nothing about this patient, her diagnosis or her emotional state. I was not prepared for the raw emotion that hung like a fog in the room as I entered. This young lady was 28 years old; she was married and had three very young children. As I cheerfully said hello and asked how she was that beautiful afternoon, I was met with a smorgasbord of emotional responses. I explained to her that I was a hospital chaplain and just wanted to encourage her as she recovered from her surgery. I have to let the reader know that at this point in my ministry, I had not taken any units of Clinical Pastoral Education. If I had, I would have been much more prepared for the events that were about to happen.

This young lady had just been informed that she had stage four cancer and any treatment for her condition at this point would not be very beneficial. She was coping with the realization that the life she had planned, raising her children and building a home with her loving husband, would not be as she imagined it. This young lady was a very devout Christian.

She was progressing through the steps of grief and was stalled in the area of anger and blame. She was mad at herself for letting her children down and not being there to raise them and she was mad at God for allowing this to happen. She loudly cried out, "How could God do this? Doesn't He know my children need me? Chaplain, why is God allowing this to happen to me? I'm a good person and I have always been faithful to Him - tell me, why?"

She was pleading with me as though the answer to "why" would drive away her hurt and anger and give her some sense of reason. I stood in the center of the room that day and felt her anguish and pain. I had no answer to share, no encouraging words that would calm her grief. Of course, I used the coined words that many Christians use to justify suffering and loss. However, to me at that moment, they sounded hollow and empty. She had now calmed down and was holding my hand and as I looked into her eyes I saw the feelings of betrayal and hurt as her faith in God stood challenged by her diagnosis and prognosis of future decline and suffering. As she realized that her arms would soon not hold her children, she could almost hear their cries for their dying mother's attention.

That visit challenged my own spiritual foundation as I asked myself why I did not have an answer for something so prevalent and real, all around me, in this hospital. I was skilled in Bible doctrine and I had acquired knowledge but I could not draw wisdom on how to apply what I already knew. I was determined that day to never be caught off guard again like I was that day.

As a minister I felt it was my responsibility to have an answer to every question. I immediately tried to find the answer in books. I remember purchasing a book, "Why Do Bad Things Happen to Good People?" The more I read the more I realized the answers I was seeking were as empty as the ones I had been using.

This event took place nearly 36 years ago. During this time I have greatly increased my preparation in this area as a chaplain. This scene has been played out many times throughout the years. There are no coined answers that can be used for every problem. Each person on earth is unique and their life and journey is unique as well. That thought hit home a number of years ago when I was reading from St. Paul's last letter to Timothy before his death.

> *"I have fought a good fight, I have finished my course, I have kept the faith: [8] Henceforth there is laid up for me a crown of righteousness, which the Lord, the righteous judge, shall give me at that day: and not to me only, but unto all them also that love his appearing." (2 Timothy 4:7-8, KJV)*

Even though I have read this scripture numerous times, the words "*finished my course*", seemed to jump off the page. What did Paul mean, "finished my course?" It was then that I began to realize just as a river follows its course to an ocean, no river's course is exactly the same. Thus, it would be foolish for me to think every person's course would also be the same. That is why the scripture tells us to not compare ourselves among ourselves.

> *"For we dare not class ourselves or compare ourselves with those who commend themselves. But they, measuring themselves by themselves, and comparing themselves among themselves, are not wise."* (2 Corinthians 10:12, KJV)

Thus I began to understand that each person's course is different and fits into the plan of God for humanity. Each person has been given specific talents and abilities that will be beneficial to fulfill their role on earth. Think about how different siblings can be in their abilities and personalities. Just as unique as they are in their talents and abilities, so are they different in their span of life. Some have short spans and others long. Each person follows their own course. As each snowflake that falls to earth is different from another, so each life is different and is presented with its own set of blessings and challenges. Remember, there's only one of you in this world and your life adds something special to those you come in contact with daily.

The important thing to remember is that every person should use their gifts to fulfill their role here on earth to the best of their ability. You must be certain not to compare your talents or your circumstances to those of another.

I remember doing that very thing some time ago. It seemed my life had been filled with all sorts of challenges, most of these being health-related. I seemed to go from disease to disease and from surgery to surgery. I, at one point, asked God, "How is it, Lord, that my brother and I come from the same parents yet he has very few challenges in this area and I seem to be challenged every other day?" I actually began to think that when my mother was pregnant with me she must have been experimenting with drugs! Of course, I know that's ridiculous! Just look at identical twins who, other than their external appearance, are totally different in their personality, likes and dislikes - each created exclusively by God for His specific purpose!

I was finally coming to the realization that God placed me on earth for His purpose and had a very unique plan for my life. I may not have chosen this path personally but now, even at my weakest, I understand I can dramatically impact the lives of others I come in contact with every day. This young girl with a stage four cancer diagnosis never realized how this one visit affected my ministry and neither do you realize how your actions, attitudes and responses affect the faith and lives of those with whom you interact.

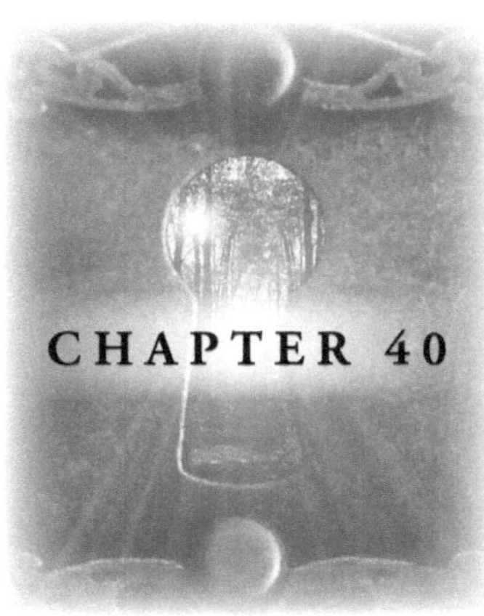

ARE YOU LOST IN THE WOODS?

I remember a number of years ago, actually it feels like an entire lifetime ago, my parents lived in a bedroom community of Milwaukee called Oak Creek. It was in the country and to the south of our home was the flowing Root River surrounded by dense woods. It was a very pastoral place where my parents would often walk together. I was probably around six years old at the time and on this particular morning, they decided to bring me along with them. I can clearly remember many of the incidents that were to occur this day because they left a lasting impression on my life.

There were just a few nondescript trails that led through the heavy underbrush. However, when one reached the river it seemed like the dense canopy opened up to reveal the clarity of a late morning sky. I had no problem following mom and dad through the thick brush but when we reached the river it seemed like the world opened up and there were countless areas for me to explore.

I took advantage of my parents' preoccupation with the beauty of the river to explore farther ahead, always wanting to see what was beyond the next bend. This was a great experience, I thought, running wild amidst the trees and foliage. I should say it was fun until I realized that I didn't know where my parents were, much less the way back to where I started. My countless cries out for them went unanswered and the longer I shouted the more panicked I became.

I began to run in search of them but little did I know I was actually running away from the spot where they had been. The river now looked completely different; it looked threatening and scary! It seemed now that all the shadows were trying to reach out and pull me in. I had none of these feelings when I was with my parents, but now I was alone and I realized the extent of my own weakness and vulnerability.

No matter how loud I cried or how many tears I shed, it seemed that fear was surrounding me and I had no way to escape. This experience left a very deep scar in my memory because I was lost for hours and hours. My parents did get help and others started to search for me. Of course, in their mind, they pictured the river claiming another victim. The more frantic I became, the deeper I felt the separation from help and security. After some time had passed, I had no more tears to cry and it seemed no one was responding to my pleas for help.

I mention this story for a reason for it is similar to most of our own personal journeys through life. The woods represent the clutter that surrounds us; each tree is like a problem that blocks our view of where we are. The brush is obscuring what lies ahead in our lives, blocking the assistance that we are seeking. At times we run ahead of God and start to give way to our childish whims in search of a more exciting place to explore. We may wander away from God and from the support and protection He provides, not to mention the guidance that He gives us. When this happens we become full of fear and things which at one time were not terrifying, now seem to close in on us and block our way to peace.

We can handle a few trees around us and a little brush but what happens if the trees become a forest and the brush is so high that we cannot see above it? It forces us to cry out for help as we realize that we cannot find our way back to where we once were. After a time we give up trying to find our way back and surrender to hopelessness as we sit in despair and question how such a beautiful day could turn into such a tragedy.

That, my friend, is exactly what happened to me that day. I had run out of energy to keep searching and I had run out of tears to keep crying. I sat in a childish stupor not knowing what else to do as night began to settle around me. It was then in the dusk of the day that a man appeared and took me by the hand and led me out. At the time I never thought of angels and their existence. I never considered that God had placed a guardian angel in my life. How grateful I was for his hand in mine. How secure I felt as hope returned that I would not forever be lost in the forest.

My parents never even met this man who led me to the road which led me home and that was where my parents found me. I expected strong words of correction and possibly a more physical punishment. However, my parents smothered me with love and affection and I learned the lesson to never give heed to wandering lusts which might lead me away from the security and comfort of my home and family.

Is it possible at this moment in your life that you are surrounded by a forest of struggles? Are the cares of life, like the thick brush, so tall that you cannot find your way home? Is it a diagnosis that blocks your view of a God who loves you? Are your emotions running wild in search of a way out but when push comes to shove, you find yourself even more desperate for a way out of your frightful situation? Have you given up? Are you emotionally drained? Have you surrendered to your situation?

There is quite possibly a hand reaching out to take yours at this very moment, leading you to a familiar place where you can once again be restored. You may feel like you're the lost sheep and the flock has moved on to greener pastures. You are sitting alone in a most frightful place at the mercy of the wolves and beasts. Let God take your hand in His and lead you back to His house, for everything you need to face at night is there to give you support.

WHEN THE MOUSE BECOMES AN ELEPHANT...FACING FEAR

Some time ago someone asked me what an elephant was. I figured it was a trick question but was surprised when he told me that an elephant is a mouse that is built to government specs. Oftentimes we can take something so small and build it into something so large that we can no longer handle it. We cannot get around it or over it and it blocks our view. It intimidates us and the sad part of this scenario is that we created this "elephant" ourselves in our own minds.

In this generation fear has become the elephant in many people's lives. This shouldn't surprise us because the scripture tells us that fear would play a major role during the time we live in.

> "*Men's hearts failing them for fear, and for looking after those things which are coming on the earth:*" (Luke 21:26, KJV)

The definition of fear according to Webster's Dictionary: FEAR, *noun* 1. A painful emotion or passion excited by an expectation of evil or the apprehension of impending danger.

During Franklin D. Roosevelt's Inaugural Address in 1932, the Nation was still reeling from the Great Depression. He addressed a frightened nation and spoke these words:

> "This great Nation will endure as it has endured, will revive and will prosper. So, first of all, let me assert my firm belief that the only thing we have to fear is fear itself—nameless, unreasonable, unjustified terror which paralyzes needed efforts to convert retreat into advance."

He referred to fear as nameless, unreasonable and unjustified. Yet fear is so powerful when allowed to run within the walls of our lives without restraint that it can paralyze us and drive us into the cavern of despair and depression.

I was told at one time that a lion roars just before its attack to gain an advantage over its prey. So frightened is the animal, that for a moment, it hesitates in pure panic. This gives the lion an advantage in his attack.

Now I, no doubt, am speaking to some who have been held in the grips of fear and felt its terror and restraint. Some, at this moment, may themselves be shaking their head in agreement. The scripture plainly declares this:

> "*There is no **fear** in love; but perfect love casteth out **fear**: because **fear hath torment**. He that **fear**eth is not made perfect in love.*" (1 John 4:18, KJV)

Fear has torment; it hinders your perspective of God. It restrains the Gifts of the Spirit from operating in your heart, Love, Joy, Peace..... and so on. It is possible to experience fear and not even know why it is present. The scripture actually refers to this type of fear as the spirit of fear. It is good to note that this type of fear was never intended to cripple a Christian's life. Note the following scripture:

> "*For God has not given us a spirit of fear, but of power and of love and of a sound mind.*" (2 Timothy 1:7, KJV)

The question then lies in our lap. If God never gave us this fear we are dealing with, it must be coming from another source. I look closely at this scripture and I see that God gives us power, love and a sound mind - but not fear! I think I could say then, with a little liberty, that when we are experiencing fear we do not have a sound mind. Now I have owned horses for a good part of my life and when someone tells me a horse is sound I am hearing that the horse has no physical defect, or for that matter, mental defect.

If I, as a Christian, am sound, I can assume everything mentally and physically is functioning as it was intended. What causes us to become defective? Some type of injury comes to my mind first. Mental injury or physical injury, both can damage our functionality. Somehow, somewhere, we have picked up something or have been affected by something that has left a mark on the way we think or feel.

Somehow I feel qualified to talk on this subject from my own experiences. That is why this topic is so important for us to understand. Fear can cripple us physically and emotionally and God most certainly does not want us to live with fear in any form. I found out that it is one thing to know the scriptures and another to put them to work in our lives.

Some time ago I had major surgery, one of many surgeries in my life. I had already been conditioned by past experiences that went awry and so when this one ran into difficulties afterward, fear was pounding on the door of my mind. It was not mere trepidation but it was a full-blown agonizing and paralyzing fear. It was, to say the least, overwhelming and I anguished over the fact that I, as a Christian, was experiencing something that I felt showed my lack of faith in God. I prayed for it to go away but like a bulldog holding onto a bone, it would not let go no matter how hard I prayed and wanted it to leave. I had an immense amount of pain and with the pain came nausea and anxiety. I actually thought that I would die. I tried to distract myself from the fear by trying to keep my mind on other things. However, that lasted only for a short period of time. I remember one day asking God why I was being so tormented. "Lord, please I cried, I do not want to deal with this fear any longer." I tried casting it out in Jesus' Name but nothing happened. At that moment I discovered I certainly was not sound in my faith in this area.

The following scripture came to my mind one morning:

> "*There is no fear in love; but perfect love casteth out fear: because fear hath torment. He that feareth is not made perfect in love.*" (1 John 4:18, KJV)

I began to contemplate on what the real foundation of love is and realized that the core of love is built on trust. Without trust, love cannot survive. I loved God but did I trust Him? I began to ask myself questions like, "Can you remember a time when God absolutely failed you?" I could remember times when my prayers were not speedily answered, but they were answered. I could not think of one time in my life when God failed me. He had always come through and even used the bad things in my life to produce blessings in my future. My answer was simple and crystal clear. I needed to fully place my trust in God to carry me through.

I remember my dad playing helicopter with me as a little boy. He would grab one hand and one foot and spin me around higher and higher. I would squeal in joy knowing that no matter how dizzy or frightening this may have been, he would never let me go. I actually looked forward to those times. I then remembered this verse in God's Word:

> "*Now unto him that is able to keep you from falling, and to present you faultless before the presence of his glory with exceeding joy,* [25] *To the only wise*

> *God our Saviour, be glory and majesty, dominion and power, both now and ever. Amen*" (Jude 24-25, KJV)

I began to realize that no matter how crazy, no matter how painful, no matter how lonely I felt, that God was holding onto me and would never let me go to suffer lasting harm. I guess there are a lot of Christians just like me. They love God but when push comes to shove many find out that their level of trust only goes so far.

> *"Trust in the LORD with all thine heart; and lean not unto thine own understanding.* [6] *In all thy ways acknowledge him, and he shall direct thy paths."* (Proverbs 3:5,6, KJV)

We need to trust Him completely and learn to cast all of our care, all of our anxiety onto Him.

> "*Casting all your care upon him; for he careth for you.*" (1 Peter 5:7, KJV)

Now the million-dollar question: how do I cast all of my care on Him? The Lord brings to mind, as I write this, an incident that took place when I was a teenager. It was a very wet spring with many heavy rains. Rivers were overflowing their banks and roads near us were closed. A couple of us guys got together and thought it would be fun to jump off the Root River Bridge and let the current carry us downstream. We never thought about the many things that could go wrong or how we were flirting with death. We each dared the other to make the plunge.

The water was so high that year that there was only a foot between the bottom of the bridge and the water itself. The trick was to make sure that when you came up out of the water and you were under the bridge that you did not hit your head on the cement bridge's bottom. One after the other we jumped in and the current carried us away. We surrendered to its pull and it carried us down the river at a miraculous speed. Can I trust God as I trusted myself that day? Can I jump into His arms when I am afraid and let Him carry me to a place of assurance and peace showing me that He is in control and watching over me?

Sometimes it's a leap of faith but He has never let me down before and promises not to in the future.

I remember years ago a person asked me a question, "Steve, do you think one man can eat an elephant?" I said that I thought it was not possible but he went on to say, "You're wrong! One man *can* eat an elephant but he can only eat it one bite at a time." Is your struggle as large as an elephant and does it look so insurmountable that you are totally overwhelmed? Remember, there is no problem so large that it cannot be overcome if you take it one bite at a time.

RICHARD'S GETHSEMANE

I have asked my brother, Rick, to share some experiences that I feel are very relative to the topic of this book. However, before I let him share his story I must take a moment to share a few thoughts.

Rick and I were like oil and water when we were growing up. We had very little in common. He loved sports; I loved horses and the outdoors. He was always blessed with good health and I was affected by every disease that came along. I began to wonder why I was cursed with diseases like ulcerative colitis and other things too numerous to mention and he never even hardly got a cold.

We've both been in the ministry now for over 40 years and have become the best of friends and our lives are so very intertwined. I was glad that I was able to share in his struggle and it has only brought us closer together. Please open your heart as he shares his deepest thoughts with you.

My brother Steve and I were always opposites until we came to know the Lord. Even now he struggles with the physical and I with the spiritual. My greatest struggles have been in my mind and heart. We have learned to help each other!

My father was a WWII prisoner. At a young age he became a smoker. By the time he was 48 he had half of one lung removed, and was near death from lung cancer. My brother Steve, my wife Liz and I, came to Parkway Apostolic Church in 1973 and our lives were forever changed. My parents (Richard and Dorothy) as well as my sister, Linda, all began our Jesus relationship together. Seeing my dad suffer from cancer scared me off from ever smoking. My dad received a miracle healing upon his new relationship and was cancer free for 11 years! He died at the age of 59.

As I approached my 55th birthday, a spirit of fear spoke to my mind, "You will die of cancer, you will die young, and you will suffer greatly." I immediately asked God to tell me this wasn't so. God went silent. For the next 40 days that spirit repeated the same speech, and as often as I asked God to tell me it wasn't so, He remained silent. The fear, worry, and anxiety of this trial were overwhelming! I finally realized I needed to hear from God. "Tell me what I need to hear, even if it's not what I want to hear."

Then God spoke, "Before I answer your question, I want you to answer mine. Have I failed you in the past?" I responded, "No sir!" "Then why would you think I'd fail you in the future? I won't tell you if you'll die young, die of cancer, or suffer greatly, but I will tell you, whatever you go through, I will be right there with you, and I will give you what you need when you need it." That's the moment the trial ended!

Never tell God what to say. Trust God for what you need, thank God for what you have or had. The trial I faced lasted 40 days. Just as Goliath preached the same message for 40 days – so this trial lasted 40 days, until one boy and a Great God stood against an inferior giant.

At the age of 56, I had kidney stones - the worst pain I have ever experienced! I couldn't afford insurance, but I did have a major medical plan. The deductible was $5,000! I had been told previously to have a colonoscopy by age 50. I did not because I couldn't afford it, but now that I had used up my deductible, I thought I might as well "get it done".

The test revealed that I had a tumor in my colon. The doctor didn't think it was cancerous so he referred me to my family doctor. My brother Steve has had his own giants in the form of health issues. He is also excellent at helping others through sickness and even hospice. I asked Steve if he would join me at the doctor's office to hear what was next. I was so glad he came. When the Doctor came in, he seemed in a good mood. Then he put the hammer down, "You have a cancerous tumor against the wall of your colon. It is too large to remove. You will need chemo and radiation to shrink the tumor, followed by a 4-6 hour surgery. You will then wear a colostomy bag for at least six months. You will also be examined throughout your body for other areas of cancer. If we find it in your lymph nodes, all bets are off. If you would have waited 6 more months we wouldn't be able to help you at all." I immediately burst into tears.

My life is over. How can I even look at my wife, family and friends without falling on the ground and weeping? My brother Steve held my hand (so to speak); he encouraged me in the Lord. I was so glad he was there! The day of the Doctor's announcement was December 21, 2007. The trial would last for another 40 days. No cancer was found anywhere else in my body. I decided I would take one phase of this trial at a time.

Chemotherapy was my only target. Would I be sick all the time? Would I become weak? Would my immune system be weakened so that I could catch something else? The day finally arrived. When I met the oncologist, I thought I was ready. His only job was to give me chemo. Before he did, he looked at me and said, "I don't feel comfortable giving you chemotherapy." He then referred me to a specialist at the University of Wisconsin Hospital in Madison, Wisconsin. The doctors at UW wanted to see if they could remove the tumor without chemo and radiation.

We prepared for surgery. Before the surgery my insurance company said they wouldn't pay for it because I was out of network! The greatest battles are fought between your two ears. Either your eyes or humanistic thinking can spread your fears. Fear is torment. "You'll lose everything, your home and savings." I appealed to the insurance company. I reminded them of the savings from no chemo or radiation. I asked them to "prayerfully" consider their position. God moved on them, and the bill was "paid in full!"

The surgery was a success! Tumor removed! Bills paid! God is good – all the time! First of all, I want to thank Jesus! I also want to thank my brother Steve for being such an encourager, our church (Abundant Life) for their prayers and friendship, and the doctors and nurses whom God used. Without that kidney stone, I would have never known about my colon cancer. "All things work together for good!" To God be the Glory – Great things He has done!

I will forever be thankful for the many miracles God has done for me during this cancer trial! When the trials were over, I asked God a question, "Why?" His answer was this – "This was for my Glory and your testimony. When you hear of someone who gets cancer you won't sympathize, you will empathize." You now have another field to work in! To God be the Glory – let my testimony be an encouragement.

CHAPTER 43

YOU ARE NOT ALONE

As Christians, we at times may forget to whom we belong and the relationship that God has ordained for us to have with Him. In Acts 17 these words are recorded for our admonition and guidance:

> *"God that made the world and all things therein, seeing that he is Lord of heaven and earth, dwelleth not in temples made with hands; [25] Neither is worshipped with men's hands, as though he needed anything, seeing he giveth to all life, and breath, and all things; [26] And hath made of one blood all nations of men for to dwell on all the face of the earth, and hath determined the times before appointed, and the bounds of their habitation;*
>
> *[27] That they should seek the Lord, if haply they might feel after him, and find him, though he be not far from every one of us: [28] For in him we live, and move, and have our being; as certain also of your*

> *own poets have said, For we are also his offspring.* [29] *Forasmuch then as we are the offspring of God, we ought not to think that the Godhead is like unto gold, or silver, or stone, graven by art and man's device.* [30] *And the times of this ignorance God winked at; but now commandeth all men everywhere to repent:* (Acts 17:24-30, KJV)

This scripture boldly declares that as a "born again" child of God I am the offspring of God. It reminds me that I should not try to compare that relationship to my surroundings or things ordained by mere mortal men, as stated above in verse 29.

John carries on this thought in 1 John:

> "*Beloved, now are we the sons of God, and it doth not yet appear what we shall be: but we know that, when he shall appear, we shall be like him; for we shall see him as he is.*" (1 John 3:2, KJV)

John is encouraging those who are facing trials and tribulations that there is a destiny for those who are faithful in affliction. Paul states this even more clearly in Romans 8:

> "*And if children, then heirs; heirs of God, and joint-heirs with Christ; if so be that we suffer with him, that we may be also glorified together.*" (Romans 8:17, KJV)

The scripture, in relation to suffering, never exempts the believer from trials and hardship. Quite to the contrary, it identifies our suffering with that of Christ. Jesus relates this to His disciples before His ascension.

> "*Then said Jesus unto his disciples, If any man will come after me, let him deny himself, and take up*

> *his cross, and follow me.* [25] *For whosoever will save his life shall lose it: and whosoever will lose his life for my sake shall find it.*" (Matthew 16:24-25, KJV)

Now, none of these thoughts sound real appealing, but Christ is expressing to His followers that He expects, from them, the same commitment that He is making with them. As part of the family of God, I will be expected to make the same sacrifices as every other member. When we ate a meal at home growing up, we all ate the same meal. Whether it was hamburgers or steak we all partook of the same thing. If the world has hated Christ, you can expect it to hate you because you cannot dissect one portion of a family from another; we all bear the same Name.

Now going back to where we first started, Luke records in Acts 17:30 that in times past God winked at our ignorance but now He is commanding ALL men to repent. The word repent has an interesting definition for it means to change one's mind, to turn around and go in a different direction. Paul is even clearer on this subject in Romans 12:

> "*And be not conformed to this world: but be ye transformed by the renewing of your mind, that ye may prove what is that good, and acceptable, and perfect, will of God.*" (Romans 12:2, KJV)

He refers to repentance as a transformed mind that has been renewed to its original state. This way we will know what is good and acceptable and in the will of God. So let's put it this way: we as Christians have two minds, one is the carnal mind which minds the things of the flesh and then there is the spiritual mind that minds things that are of God or the Spirit. Now depending on which mind we are using at the time will determine how easy it will be for us to comprehend the will of God. The earthly mind does not comprehend the things of the Spirit; it's great at detecting what's going on in the realm of our fleshly experiences but it focuses more on satisfying its own needs and not so much those things that are profitable to the spiritual side of our life. Paul firmly states this in Romans 8:

> "*Because the carnal mind is enmity against God: for it is not subject to the law of God, neither indeed can be.* [8] *So then they that are in the flesh cannot please God.*" (Romans 8:7-8, KJV)

Notice that our carnal or fleshly thoughts are not profitable in the spiritual realm for they rebel against or reject the spiritual laws of God. In the realm of carnal thinking, it is impossible to connect with God in a way that would please Him. The flesh is more concerned about itself than it is about following spiritual instruction and divine fellowship.

Now I focus on this topic for a reason. If you are trying to understand why events are transpiring in your life the way that they are currently happening, you will want to make sure you are looking at them through the right lens. Also make sure you are using the right mind, spiritual or carnal, to understand why these events are happening and where they may lead you.

Paul in Philippians calls that spiritual mind the mind of Christ:

> "*Let this mind be in you, which was also in Christ Jesus:* [6] *Who, being in the form of God, thought it not robbery to be equal with God:* [7] *But made himself of no reputation, and took upon him the form of a servant, and was made in the likeness of men:* [8] *And being found in fashion as a man, he humbled himself, and became obedient unto death, even the death of the cross.*" (Philippians 2: 5-8, KJV)

This is the type of thinking that gets you through the storms of trials and suffering. It sees the end from the beginning and produces faith and peace amidst fear and agony. Instead of looking in the mirror of life and seeing yourself, you see Christ and His plan for you as well as what is prepared for you in the future.

I find it quite interesting in the miracle of the loaves and fishes how Jesus tests His disciples to see which mind they would use.

> "*After these things Jesus went over the sea of Galilee, which is the sea of Tiberias.* [2] *And a great multitude followed him, because they saw his miracles which he did on them that were diseased.* [3] *And Jesus went up into a mountain, and there he sat with his disciples.* [4] *And the Passover, a feast of the Jews, was nigh.* [5] *When Jesus then lifted up his eyes, and saw a great company come unto him, he saith unto Philip, Whence shall we buy bread, that these may eat?* [6] *And this he said to prove him: for he himself knew what he would do.*" (John 6:1-6, KJV)

Now Phillip looked at it through the fleshly mind and manner of thinking and said there was no way they could feed so many people. Even if they had 200 pennyworth which would equal 200 denarii they still could not give everyone more than just a morsel to eat. One denarius in Bible times was equal to a day's wage. Your fleshly mind tells you that this is not probable or even possible. Your spiritual mind knows that God's math is not man's math. He takes a little boy's lunch and multiplies it in His hands and feeds over five thousand people and still has 12 baskets full of leftovers. Now balancing your checkbook is alright for using human reasoning or thinking but when it comes to God's plans for your life you will have to use a renewed mind. Rest assured God will test you in different circumstances to see which mind you use to solve your problems. God likes to prove us; it is not only so that we can know what we are capable of but to allow us to know what He can do in our circumstances. God does some of His greatest miracles through the most unlikely sources.

For many of us it is a journey we have to take; it's realizing that we are really never in complete control and our own abilities and knowledge are far from adequate when we face the trials of life. God has a way of letting us learn just how in control we are. It is not that He wants us to live with feelings of inadequacy. It is that He wants us to learn where our true strength comes from.

> "*Not that I speak in respect of want: for I have learned, in whatsoever state I am, therewith to be content.* [12] *I know both how to be abased, and I know how to abound: everywhere and in all things I am instructed both to be full and to be hungry, both to abound and to suffer need.* [13] *I can do all things through Christ which strengtheneth me.*" (Philippians 4:11-13, KJV)

The testing ground of proving is the place where we learn what God can do and what we cannot. I guess I might be classified as a typical guy when it comes to buying a car. I like to take a test drive. I like to see how the car handles and what it can and cannot do. I have been known to put the pedal to the metal on an entrance ramp to an Interstate to see how much power is under the hood. I need to know this because if I were to buy the car there might be a time that I would need that power to merge with traffic. God allows us to experience trials in our lives so we know what He can do. Whether it is just a test drive or a major merge into congested traffic, the knowledge of our previous tests will give us the confidence to face what's at the end of the ramp of our lives.

It is interesting to note that the proving ground that often lies in front of us and tests our relationship is also used in like manner to prove God and His promises. Look at Malachi 3:

> "*Bring ye all the tithes into the storehouse, that there may be meat in mine house, and prove me now herewith, saith the Lord of hosts, if I will not open you the windows of heaven, and pour you out a blessing, that there shall not be room enough to receive it.*" (Malachi 3:10, KJV)

See, the Lord says, if I will not bless you, proving His promises are true. It seems that as a Christian I am constantly standing on promises and commitments that God has given to me to provide a base for growth and wisdom through experience.

The three Hebrew children were not afraid to enter into the furnace of judgment for their faith and commitment to God's commands. They had already seen God prove Himself to them in so many ways previously that they trusted Him with their lives no matter the outcome. This spiritual battle on the plains of Babylon was not won at the moment that it presented itself; it was won a long time before in a renewed and spiritual mindset. Notice what they tell the king when he gives them a chance to change their mind before he burns them to death:

> "*Shadrach, Meshach, and Abednego, answered and said to the king, O Nebuchadnezzar, we are not careful to answer thee in this matter.* [17] *If it be so, our God whom we serve is able to deliver us from the burning fiery furnace, and he will deliver us out of thine hand, O king.* [18] *But if not, be it known unto thee, O king, that we will not serve thy gods, nor worship the golden image which thou hast set up.*" (Daniel 3:16-18, KJV)

Our victories are often preceded by the proving grounds of previous trials.

Sometimes God sends us out upon the sea of life and allows life's storms to overtake us. Then He comes walking upon the water and takes us by the hand and carries us to safety. You can choose to stay in the boat like so many others or you can reach out your hand and walk upon the unknown waters. You can feel the peace that God provides through the storm that might be raging in your life at this very moment. In Christ, you will find a safe haven to rest while the storm rages around you.

There is no limit to what God can or will do for you in your time of trial. He has been known to make the sun stand still for almost a full day for Joshua as he faced his enemies. He opened the earth to swallow Moses's accusers. He provided water from a rock in the wilderness for Israel. It does not matter if He heals you miraculously or through the hands of a doctor. There is no pit you can fall into that He cannot pull you out of, no prison so secure that He will not send an angel to release you as He did with Peter. He can send ravens to bring you food in the midst of a famine as He did with Elijah and He does all these things because He is helplessly in love with you. So hold on, my friend, and expect the unexpected!

If you are in a battle today against a stronghold in your life and you can find no way around its walls and the enemy is hunkered down amidst the stronghold, let the Captain of the Lord's host lead you in the confrontation that withholds you from receiving His promises. You will see the walls will fall flat and you will go forward into a new area of possibilities and potential.

Just remember, it has to be God's way and not yours. Oftentimes the battle doesn't make sense, but God is shaking the foundation of the enemy's spiritual barricade and soon the walls will fall flat and you will walk in to take possession of what God has prepared for you in a land of promise and provision.

There is no enemy or obstacle that can separate you from the love of God!

> "*Nay, in all these things we are more than conquerors through him that loved us.* [38] *For I am persuaded, that neither death, nor life, nor angels, nor principalities, nor powers, nor things present, nor things to come,* [39] *Nor height, nor depth, nor any other creature, shall be able to separate us from the love of God, which is in Christ Jesus our Lord.*" (Romans 8; 37-39, KJV)

www.ingramcontent.com/pod-product-compliance
Lightning Source LLC
Chambersburg PA
CBHW021357150726
47989CB00005B/2289
9798653840463